SPECIAL CHILDREN, SPECIAL NEEDS

SPECIAL CHILDREN, SPECIAL NEEDS

Families talk about mental handicap

Mary McCormack

Thorsons
An Imprint of HarperCollins*Publishers*

Thorsons
An Imprint of HarperCollins*Publishers*
77–85 Fulham Palace Road,
Hammersmith, London W6 8JB

Published by Thorsons 1992
10 9 8 7 6 5 4 3 2 1

© Mary McCormack 1992

Mary McCormack asserts the moral right to
be identified as the author of this work

A catalogue record for this book
is available from the British Library

ISBN 0 7225 2598 2

Printed in Great Britain by
Billing & Sons Ltd, Worcester

Contents

Acknowledgements

I would like to thank the following individuals and organizations, for providing help and information: Linda Averall(BIMH), Birmingham Multi-Handicap Group, John Boarder, Birmingham Society for Mentally Handicapped Children and Adults, Contact a Family, Gwyn Fraser, Sheila Jupp, Martin Gallagher, Jean Richardson, Barbara Hart, Sally Doyle, Paul Thomas, Joyce Rowthorne, Carol Oviatt-Ham, PIN Group, Avon Mental Handicap Action Group, Pauline Fairbrother and the Down's Syndrome Association.

Grateful thanks also to the families, without whom the book could not have been written. It was not possible to include all the interviews, but each one played a vital role in rounding out the picture.

Foreword

I was so delighted when Mary McCormack asked me to write the foreword to this splendid new book. As both the parent of a daughter with a mental handicap, and as Chairman of MENCAP, you can imagine that I have studied and read more about the subject than most.

What makes *Special Children, Special Needs* so refreshing to me is that it literally reaches out and touches the reader with a sympathy and insight rarely found in a world of textbooks and manuals.

By following the lives of people with a mental handicap almost exclusively through the comments and observations of their families, the book builds up a first-hand account of the real trials, challenges and satisfactions that different people experience. From the often devastating worries and shock of finding out that your child is handicapped, through the early years of home and school, and on to the uncertainties of adult life, *Special Children, Special Needs* cuts through the jargon, the theory and the politics to give account after account of the love, laughter, tears and hopes of the families concerned.

The book speaks for itself, and does not inundate the reader with facts. Helpful names, addresses and phone numbers are sensibly selected and kept to a minimum. If you have a child with a mental handicap, this book will clearly call out to you that you are not alone. Your struggles and hopes are echoed by hundreds of others like you.

If you don't have any personal experience of mental handicap, read it as a story of today – a world we live in where the term 'handicap' is defined by the barriers other people put around their definition of what is normal. Change the criteria, broaden these barriers and give families the time and money they need to provide the necessary additional care, and we can abolish many of the problems currently associated with mental handicap.

The quality and quantity of help, offered to people with a mental handicap and their families, has improved tremendously, but many parents are still not receiving all the information they need to help them make vital decisions about their child's future.

This book deserves a wide readership, and will, I am sure, go far in helping that process accelerate.

Sir Brian Rix, CBE, DL
Chairman, MENCAP

Introduction

'MENTAL HANDICAP' OR 'LEARNING DIFFICULTIES'?

Throughout this book the terms 'mental handicap' and 'learning difficulties' are used interchangeably. Where people are quoted, I have used the term they used. I'm well aware that, at the time of writing, battles rage over which term is the correct one. A psychologist who runs self-advocacy groups says:

> We are encouraging people with learning difficulties to speak up for themselves. When they do we owe it to them to listen, and what they are saying is that 'mental handicap' is offensive. They say 'mental' is associated with being mad. It's become a term of abuse.

The mother of a grown-up daughter with Down's Syndrome, who also runs a mothers' group, says:

> 'Learning difficulties' is a meaningless phrase and I've never met a parent who didn't agree. To most people it suggests someone with dyslexia or maybe a child in what they used to call a remedial class at school. It trivializes the severity of the problems most of our kids have, and the public, who we expect to make donations, don't know what we're talking about.

The Secretary of a MENCAP group explained how she deals with the tricky issue: 'I say "mental handicap" when I'm talking to parents and "learning difficulties" when I'm with professionals.' Well, yes, me too. It's called sitting on the fence.

In the twenty-five years of my son's life I've heard him described, quite properly at the time, as backward, retarded, subnormal and spastic. Not long ago, it was okay to say 'mentally handicapped child', then, under the 'people first' principle, it had to be 'a child with a mental handicap'. A doctor, trained in the 1950s, recalled hearing a consultant thunder the diagnosis, 'Mother, your child is a cretin.' A nurse, near retiring age, explained that during his training, text books had taught him to divide his patients (another unacceptable term) into categories of idiot, imbecile and moron. And was it really only ten years or so ago that 'mongol' was in common usage? It's likely that any name you pick will end up as a playground term of abuse, though I can see even the most inventive schoolchild having trouble adapting 'learning difficulties' to slip abusively off the tongue.

Maybe we should change names every ten years on principle, to keep ahead of the game, though this would pose all sorts of credibility problems for 'brand name' organizations like MENCAP and the Spastics Society. Even where there is general agreement that 'mental handicap' has run its course, not everyone is sure that 'learning difficulties' is the natural successor. There are other contenders, with 'learning disability' a popular, and perhaps more accurate, choice.

To many parents it's all academic. 'Quite honestly, does it matter?' asked one mother in her seventies. 'If there was a good place for my daughter to go to when I'm not here, with kind people to look after her, I wouldn't give a damn what they called her. They're only words after all.'

PATRICK

My son, Patrick, born with severe mental and physical disabilities, is 25 and lives at home. He has multiple handicaps or profound multiple learning difficulties – call it what you will. At some point between conception and a difficult birth he suffered brain damage.

He's hard to describe – a list of 'Things Patrick Can Do' would be very short, while his limitations would run off the end of the page. He cannot walk, talk, stand or feed himself and he is incontinent. But when I say this people tend to see, at worst, an inanimate object; at best, a docile, pliable being, incapable of bad traits.

Patrick is neither. He is very much a person with his own likes and dislikes, and there are many of the latter. He dislikes being taken anywhere in a wheelchair that involves stopping even briefly. He loathes being washed, shaved, having his hair and nails cut or his clothes changed. He will shriek and fight with every ounce of strength to prevent you doing these things, and many more which have to be done.

The strength of his objections bears very little relation to the discomfort suffered, and there is limited logic but great consistency to his whims. He will only allow certain people to feed him; when one of the chosen few turned up with a full dinner plate after a four-year gap, he welcomed her with a smile and meekly cooperated.

Like most people, Patrick can be irritating and boring or lovable and funny. On a good day, he is like a playful little boy who will initiate baby games which involve you ducking behind chairs or peeping at him or banging your feet or pretending to be frightened when he shouts. This reduces him to peals of laughter. On the floor or in bed he spends a lot of time looking at books and I keep him supplied with a selection of Ladybirds and Annuals. (Shocked cries of 'age inappropriate' here from professionals, who'd probably give him P.D. James or Jeffrey Archer!)

On the bad days, when he complains continually and refuses to consider the food you've carefully prepared and you can see no reason for his irritability, it is easy to lose patience, and forget that he is probably always in discomfort and often in pain, which he can't tell you about, or understand.

He has, over the years, developed a bad curvature of the spine, which is not only potentially painful in itself but restricts and affects all his inner organs. It's one of several deformities, brought on by his spasticity, that have changed Patrick drastically from the perfect-looking baby I brought home from hospital a quarter of a century ago.

If, fifteen years ago, someone had told me that Patrick would still be living at home now with no sign of moving on, I'd have been sceptical and probably horrified. In those days, I always believed that when he was a bit older he'd go to one of those lovely little residential homes, staffed by warm and wonderful houseparents that I'd heard about. It took a few years to realize that these homes from home were a myth, and that almost certainly, for someone as handicapped as Patrick, the only alternative was a residential hospital. Even that last resort is out now as hospitals close, and that much-misunderstood notion 'community care' takes a hold.

And so Patrick has stayed at home and the years have drifted by. His younger sister has grown up and gone off to university, with no visible sign of damage, though her young life was undoubtedly restricted by his presence. He was here when she arrived and he has always been part of her life, part of the furniture almost. The restrictions he imposed she accepted, mostly, as normal. She expected her friends to accept him and, mostly, they did.

When she left, I missed not so much the practical help, because she was never one of those 'little mothers', but the moral support and the brightness and liveliness she brought to the mundane tasks of caring. The first time she came home from university for the weekend, she couldn't believe the amount of noise Patrick made and the constant physical attention he needed. She had to get that far away to see it clearly.

I have never attempted to be a superwoman. As a family we cope only with a network of support. There is the day centre, far from perfect but vital to most parents. Then, for us, there is a sitting service, set up in this case by myself and two other desperate mothers of multi-handicapped sons. We take no credit for the large, professional organization this care attendant scheme has grown into, but we did start it as we meant it to go on – with a paid coordinator, and paid care attendants who would go into homes and take over the care at whatever times families needed them. Kindly volunteers who could only do the job to fit in with their own family commitments were out; so was the idea of mothers sitting for each other's handicapped children – your own is quite exhausting enough. The Birmingham Multi-Handicap group was born because we were in the right place at the right time – when, miraculously, there was grant money available – with the right idea.

The third personal strand of support network is a respite care home, which can take Patrick for a week or so in the summer and half a dozen weekends a year. At least it was. Within the last month the unit, run by a voluntary organization, where Patrick had thoroughly enjoyed short stays for several years, has stopped taking him. He is too old, and has been for a long time, though they have turned a blind eye. The local Social Services department has nothing else to offer.

So what happens now? Do we forget about holidays, put up and shut up? Do we wait for the something that's bound to turn up? Do we nag and complain, till, maybe, a place is found somewhere? And do we then, however unsuitable it is, however unhappy Patrick is there, accept it on the grounds that we need a break? Whose needs are they anyway?

It is one of those everyday crises that make a carer's life a little like taking a trot along a tightrope. You may be balancing nicely, getting rather smug even, but there's always a crisis just around the corner ready to knock you off your rope.

COPING

The proportion of people with a mental handicap in the general population is estimated at 2 per cent. Of these only one in every ten is severely affected, which gives a figure of 2–3 per thousand for adults and 3–4 per thousand for children.

Put like that it doesn't seem too big a problem, does it? But for every one of the families into which such a child is born, life will never be the same again. They are entering a world they probably didn't know existed – a world of therapists and social workers, of special education and day centres, of dashed hopes and unexpected strengths, of grief and joy.

Nobody wants to give birth to a child with a mental handicap. It is one of the worst shocks and the most devastating disappointments that life can throw at you. Yet most people love their child and come to terms with the situation. Some even learn to enjoy it. They find that life is enhanced; their child opens doors to new experiences and new friends.

It never gets easy though. Mothers talk about the way they have changed. They have 'toughened up', learned to stand up for themselves and for their child's rights. 'Nobody gives you anything. You have to fight and fight and then fight some more for every bit of help you get,' said one. When outsiders say, as they often do, 'I don't know how you cope', they are rewarded with a hollow laugh. People cope because they have to. They rarely get a choice. Developing a wry sense of humour about it all, as many parents do eventually, is one way of coping. It shields against self-pity.

Some people, often professionals, seem to believe that there are born copers – the families who look after their child with the minimum of fuss and few demands upon the welfare services – and those who are infinitely less adequate. But, on the whole, the people who cope best usually have easier children to cope with. Wouldn't you find it easier to live with Ben (p.180) or Brenda (p.138) than with Carl (p.125) or Michael (p.91)?

There always comes a point at which families can no longer cope. If our children live long enough it's bound to happen to all of us eventually. Then we have to ask someone else to take over the caring. This letting go process has always been painful for parent and for child, but an additional worry is the government's Community Care Programme, due to start in 1993.

One of the aims of this is to persuade parents to keep a son or daughter with a disability at home as long as possible – or even longer, say the cynics. There's a very real fear that residential care will be even harder to find, which Martin Gallagher, of MENCAP, thinks wrong: 'I believe that parents keep their child at home for as long as they possibly can, and whether this point is reached when the child is 5 or 50, residential services should be available to them when needed.'

We are, it seems, entering nervously into a new area of community care, in which local authorities will be able to buy-in the services they need for each individual from statutory, voluntary and private sources. Who will run these services, who will supervise and control them, and how much money will be available, are questions without answers for the moment.

Meanwhile, this book is about how families feel, cope and, sometimes, fail to cope. It is for carers who want to know about other carers, and for professionals who need to know. The interviewees, who speak for themselves, were contacted through voluntary organizations, schools, day centres and by word of mouth, in several geographical areas. Their children range in age from 10 months to 48 years.

All were generous with their time and thoughts, though mothers were perhaps more willing than fathers, some of whom found reasons to be out when I called or said very little if they stayed. Occasionally, women preferred to be interviewed without their husband present; ('He gets aggressive and angry about the subject and that makes me clam up'; 'My husband never talks about our daughter. He has no thoughts on her.'; 'I might say something he wouldn't like to hear,' were among the reasons given). The men who agreed to be interviewed were very helpful, though all but one bowed to their wife as the primary carer, the one with most to say on the matter.

1 Early Years

FINDING OUT

You may find it hard to remember the date of your child's first tooth, or even first step, but you never forget the moment you find out he or she has a handicap. For some the news comes in an early, heart-breaking message hours or days after the birth. For others it's a long drawn out agony of hope and despair, spread out over months or years.

Reams have been written on how, where and when parents should be told their child has a disability. The consensus of opinion appears to be as early as possible, as positively as possible, in private, with both parents present, by a trained specialist – and with the opportunity to come back for a second meeting. Very few parents have the presence of mind to think of the questions they'd like to ask immediately after that first shattering disclosure.

Indeed, a report by the Maternity Services Committee in 1985 suggests a series of meetings between the paediatrician and parents. It also recommends that parents should be given the opportunity to have other professionals, such as a health visitor, social worker, religious counsellor or someone from a voluntary organization, involved at this early stage. Among a further list of recommendations is that parents are given written information on their child's condition, plus the address of appropriate local voluntary organizations and the name of other families with similar children who have volunteered support.

Does it happen? Not in Somerset and Avon, where Jean Richardson carried out a study project, 'Early Diagnosis and Early Counselling' in 1989, and there's no reason to suppose other areas are different. Using a questionnaire, Jean interviewed parents of children with mental handicap/learning difficulties under the age of 20. Out of approximately eighty replies per question (not everyone answered every question) she came up with the following results:

- 6 people received written information on the diagnosis;
- 19 were told of voluntary organizations;
- 30 were put in touch with other parents;
- 51 were offered support and/or counselling (though most would have welcomed it);
- genetic counselling was broached with 13 (37 would have accepted it if offered).

And who broke the news? 60 per cent were told by a specialist or paediatrician, 15 per cent by hospital doctors, 10 per cent by a general practitioner. Other informants included a psychologist, a school medical officer, midwives, a psychiatrist and health visitors. What this means, Jean Richardson points out, is that a large number of people were not informed by a specialist with appropriate experience and training to do the job. Just over half were told with their partner present. 32 per cent heard within 24 hours, with diminishing numbers being told later, down to 6.2 per cent more than 5 years later. There's a jump to 16 per cent for parents being told within 1 year, which takes in many of the children whose condition was not obvious at birth.

The truth is that however or wherever it's done, there's no easy, painless way to hear that your baby will never grow into the perfect child of your dreams; that your life, your hopes and your plans will have to change. But there must be less distressing ways than those experienced by some of the parents I interviewed – such as the mother told bluntly by a nurse that if her newborn baby lived he would be 'a vegetable', or the young couple who were given the news in a room full of medical students, who they felt were watching with clinical interest for their reaction, or the mother who was told abruptly by a consultant that her son was severely handicapped, then turned out, without further ado, to stand bemused and weeping in a busy hospital corridor. These are not incidents from the uninformed barbaric past; all the children are under 10 years old, one is only 2.

Some of the older parents could manage a wry smile at their own bad experience. This is Joan, mother of 17-year old Nick who has Down's Syndrome, talking about the way she got the news.

He was born early in the morning and I didn't get to see him till six in the evening when they brought the babies round for us to feed.

The nurse handed me my bundle and I said, almost automatically, "He's alright then?"

"No," she said. I looked at him. He had two eyes, ten fingers. He looked fine to me.

"What's the matter with him?" I asked.

"Can't you see?" she said, rather irritably. "He's mongoloid. He's a mongol."

"Is he?" I said, dropping him back in his cot as if he was contaminated.

"You'd better tell your husband. The paediatrician will see you tomorrow," was the nurse's parting shot. Jim, my husband, came in later and I blurted it out. "Oh, God, he'll be in nappies till he's 12," he said.

Next morning I saw the paediatrician. Oh, he was a depressing man. He droned on and on about these children having slitty eyes and getting fat, and how I wouldn't be able to manage him in a few years. He droned and I howled. I saw myself with this big, fat, uncontrollable child in nappies, pushing him around in a wheelchair for the rest of his life.

There was a serious and unsurprising outcome. Joan rejected the baby. She discharged herself, leaving him in the hospital and 'tried to pretend he'd never been born'. Fortunately, she says now – for she's devoted to her sweet-natured, slim and relatively able younger son – her husband continued to visit Nick in hospital. After three weeks he persuaded her to go with him: 'I found not a monster, but an ordinary baby, bonnier than the others because he was 3 weeks older than most. I picked him up and took him home and put what the doctor had said out of my mind.'

There is evidence that the way the news is broken affects the way parents adapt and cope with the child in the long term. So why do so many doctors and nursing staff get it wrong? Because they are busy, because they can't always pick the right moment or the right place, but mainly because they are human. Psychologist Sheila Jupp, who has researched this subject, writes:

Nurses and doctors, when faced with a child with a handicap, are often disturbed. With mental handicap they experience feelings of frustration because there is no cure they can offer. Their behaviour is over-influenced by their feelings and may manifest itself as a brusque dismissal of the child and its parents instead of a sensitive handling of the situation.

Breaking this sort of news, she says, has been described from the doctor's viewpoint, as 'like performing an operation without anaesthetic', and research has shown that some staff experience feelings of shock and grief similar to that of the parents when a baby turns out to have a disability.

Barbara Hart, Head of a Child and Family Centre for pre-school children with special needs, agrees with this. She says she often has to comfort nurses and health visitors when a child born to a woman they have cared for is handicapped. So professionals have feelings too – though it may not be much consolation to parents struggling with their own emotions.

However tactful the telling, nothing can prepare you for the shock. Any normal human being in those circumstances is going to feel a range of strong emotions, from depression and anger to guilt (was it something I did/didn't do?) and, occasionally, relief, if everyone else has been refusing to acknowledge what you knew or suspected. It is pointless, and possibly psychologically damaging, to deny the pain, though I suspect a lot of us try to, for the dubious compliment of being told how well we are coping while we fall to pieces inside.

When you find out depends on the child's disability and, sometimes, on the powers of observation of the people who come into contact with her or him. With easily-recognizable conditions like Down's Syndrome, parents can be told almost immediately (though one couple I spoke to were glad the news had been kept from them for the first few days, long enough for them to bond with the baby).

This instant knowledge can sometimes trigger rejection – though usually only in the short-term. The situation with Down's babies has changed drastically in the last few years. Staff know that there is no problem in placing such a child with foster or adoptive parents and parents are made aware of this option. One couple I spoke to chose to do this initially, but it was clear that the mother felt unhappy with the decision and the baby came back to live with them within a few months.

The other way of finding out is arguably the harder – but then I speak as someone who's been through it. By the time a busy consultant at an outpatient's clinic, told me that my son was handicapped – I can't remember the exact words, only the message – he was merely confirming the obvious. In the meantime, I'd suffered 16 months on a painful see-saw of hope and despair, comparing him, unfavourably, with every small child I saw, noticing the realization in other people's eyes as they looked at him, and hoping that by some miracle the signs were wrong. It seems incredible now, remembering what Patrick was like, that I could have cherished these hopes for so long.

Parents for whom a diagnosis came later tend to divide into two broad groups: those who noticed nothing seriously wrong with the child, and those who knew from the earliest days but couldn't get anyone to take it seriously. For the latter group the admission by the medical profession that there was indeed a problem came as a relief. For Nicki, interviewed in this section, the relief of a hospital nurse watching her daughter and saying, "I see what you mean," took a weight off her shoulders and allowed her the first good night's sleep she'd had since her baby was born.

According to Barbara Hart:

An increasing number of children are being diagnosed very early. We get a lot of referrals under 6 months. This is good because it enables us to start working with them as early as possible, but it also makes it easier for parents to deny the truth. A 1-month old with special needs probably won't look much different to a baby the same age without problems. It's hard to believe, looking at your beautiful baby, that there is anything wrong, and parents do become angry and start blaming people.

Of course a diagnosis made very early *can* prove wrong. I do believe in telling parents as early as possible but I'm horrified by those professionals who want to go rushing in with reams of instruction and information and overpower the family before they have had time to adjust. You have to be honest but you also have to be sensitive. It's such an egg-shell area. There's nothing wrong with professionals admitting they are human and limited and just don't know how a child will develop. It's so often the truth.

COPING IN THE EARLY DAYS

Most parents I met had the opportunity to take their child to a child development centre, where they can see all the appropriate professionals under one roof. These centres cater for children with a range of disabilities and are mostly based in hospitals, but the one Barbara Hart manages – called the Child and Family Centre – is community-based, in a city suburb. It's a purpose-built single-storey unit, which has a main hall fitted with playthings and several small rooms where children can be seen in private by a doctor, speech therapist, psychotherapist and many others. Non-handicapped brothers and sisters can come along and play too, while mothers – and, less often, fathers – can relax and chat. This particular centre also provides useful extras, like a mothers' group and a loan scheme for the expensive sort of equipment that children soon grow out of.

Surprisingly, some mothers admitted being wary of going to such centres. One felt that the moment she stepped over the threshold, 'I was admitting I had a handicapped child, and I didn't want to get involved in the whole handicap thing.' The mother of a 10-month-old had declined to go, because she was afraid 'there would be lots of children who were severely handicapped and it would make me depressed, wondering if Luke was going to turn out like that'.

What also depressed a lot of mothers was the negative attitude they met from professionals in these very early days, usually from doctors at hospital check-ups. By concentrating on the child's problems, they squashed the parents' pleasure at any small achievement. 'Every time I went they'd tell me something else that was wrong with her. It really got me down,' one mother complained. These women certainly didn't want to be told lies, but perhaps too much medical truth, piled on relentlessly, was hard to accept. What they wanted was encouragement and a little hope.

A trusted professional calling to the house regularly can provide this. She or he can offer friendship, encouragement, advice and a shoulder to cry on if necessary. Anne, interviewed in this section, spoke gratefully of the health visitor who 'allowed' her to cry when she couldn't let go in front of her family for fear of upsetting them further.

It was Anne, too, who recalled a visiting teacher accidentally telling her the name of her son's condition, something the medical specialist had omitted to mention, or she'd failed to take in: 'The teacher was working with Michael one day. "These children with cerebral palsy . . ." she began to say, and I thought, "So that's what he's got!"'

It's not unusual for parents to be left without a textbook label for their child's condition beyond, 'backward' or 'slow developer'. It was two years before the term 'brain damage', as applied to my son, entered my vocabulary, and a little longer before a G.P. who didn't mince his words described him as 'a bad spastic' and gave me the clue that Patrick too had cerebral palsy.

Sometimes a pigeon hole just can't be found – the child simply has unspecified learning difficulty or mental handicap – and this causes a lot of distress to young parents. They have a strong need to know what the condition is called, when and how it happened, what exactly went wrong – often unanswerable questions. The time the questions should be asked and asked again is when a couple want to have more children, and have any suspicion that the condition could be genetic or the damage caused by a birth or pregnancy problem that could recur.

Ironically, although there are far more early services, benefits, and sources of help available to parents than a decade ago, many still don't hear of them until their child goes to school or they meet other parents. Rather than being given information in some organized fashion, they seem to stumble on it by chance, often belatedly. There's a strong case for every maternity hospital, child development centre and G.P. presenting all parents of special needs children with a list of welfare benefits and help agencies. Some carer's groups already devise excellent local carer's packs, which are relevant to all disabled people and their carers.

Some parents feel that nothing the professionals can tell them could match talking to other parents who'd been through the same experience, and the voluntary organizations can provide parent contacts very promptly when asked. But not all parents want to be with others in the same boat. Voluntary organizations like local MENCAP groups are very concerned at the dearth of young parents joining them. Many guesses as to why are hazarded: welfare benefits and statutory provision are better, so families no longer feel the need to fundraise or pressure government; children with a mental handicap are widely accepted, so special social functions for parents and children don't have much appeal; or, they just prefer staying home and watching telly!

One middle-class couple did admit, rather shamefacedly, that it took them a while to join the Down's Syndrome Association because they feared the other members 'might not be like us'. They also admitted to being proved wrong and finding a wide cross-section of people they got on well with. Another mother said: 'I've joined our local MENCAP group and I appreciate their newsletters. I buy raffle tickets and that but I just don't have the time to go out raising funds. I don't really want to hang around with other parents of handicapped children. It's like a ghetto and you have to live in the real world.'

One of the problems with the real world is that a child with an obvious handicap is still a little unusual, and people are curious. They stare and ask questions, and however sympathetic the interest, this can cause misery to some parents. I've met mothers who confessed to disguising their child's disability, in the early days, in inventive ways. One used to prop her floppy daughter up in a pushchair, with a packet of washing powder strategically placed under each arm; another wrapped her little girl in a large fluffy scarf – even in summer – so that there was little of her face showing. They grew out of it or hardened up, as no doubt will Nicki, interviewed in this section (p.41), whose life is made miserable by people staring.

The other painful, everyday reality, is other people's children, particularly those the same age and sex as your handicapped child. Suddenly the world is full of them all fast-track developers, in direct contrast to your own child whose development plods slowly along. Several mothers described the pain – and sometimes resentment and jealousy – of watching other children progress while theirs lagged behind. And the awful, unanswerable self-pity of 'Why me? Why us? It's not fair.'

STARTING SCHOOL

Many children with special needs start school at the age of 2 or 3, though some parents choose to send them part-time initially or to keep them at home longer. There's a lot to be said for this early schooling. It gives children a degree of early stimulation and multi-disciplinary help it would be hard for any parent to match at home. And it also gives mothers a chance to catch their breath, and a little more time to spend with a younger child if there is one.

Before starting school, children with special needs are assessed by their local education authority, and 'statemented'. This means that representations from parents, medical, psychological and education specialists are taken into account and a Statement of Special Educational Needs made. This will indicate the type of provision the child needs, and name a school which can provide this.

Statements have been criticized on the grounds that the educational psychologists who write them sometimes only recommend facilities that they know are available. For instance, it might be obvious that a child would benefit greatly from speech therapy every day, but if a speech therapist is only available once a week, the latter recommendation is what will appear.

Parents are given the opportunity to appeal against a child being statemented at all (i.e. being identified as in need of Special Education), or they can appeal if they disagree with the content of the statement. The appeal committee does not have the power to overturn the decision of the education authority, but it does ensure that any disagreement is independently examined.

PORTAGE

For many children education begins even earlier. They have the chance of pre-school education from a Portage home-teacher. The scheme takes its name from the rural area of Wisconsin, U.S.A., where it was developed 20 years ago. The secret of its success is probably the fact that it takes place in the comfort of the home and makes the parent the key contributor to the child's development.

It works like this. A child with learning difficulties (or any special need) is referred to the local Portage worker – who may be employed by a local authority, a health service or a voluntary organization. She (they are overwhelmingly female) visits the family, explains the system and goes through a checklist based on normal development to discover what stage the child is at.

It is an exhaustive list that covers social development, language, motor skills, cognitive and self-help skills. After the child's level of skill in each area is assessed, the Portage worker decides, with the parent, on a new skill that should be practised and mastered before the next visit. Parent and child work at it every day and, hopefully, crack it in a week. Then it's on to something else.

Those are the bare bones of it, but in a good relationship the teacher becomes almost a family friend. Sally Doyle works with children with learning difficulties in a scheme funded by Barnardo's. She is often the first professional families get to know and, depending on the age at referral, she may be a regular weekly visitor for over two years. She meets parents who are distraught over a recent diagnosis and need a great deal of encouragement to regain hope and start work – and those who are desperately keen to start.

'I always try to be positive,' she says. 'I concentrate on what the child can do instead of what he can't. Sometimes parents have encountered very negative attitudes from other professionals. But we are realistic. We don't demand too much of a child. Goals can be broken down into very small units, but sometimes even then, a child with very severe handicaps may not manage anything. If that happens I look for another way round it. If the mother isn't getting anywhere with a particular goal I'll leave it for a while and move on to something else.'

I watched Sally at work with 10-month-old Luke, described as having some developmental delay. He's a plump, bonny baby who's just started to sit up. It is Sally's third visit. The goal during the past week has been to get Luke to take small objects out of a basket. Sally has brought a selection of brightly coloured plastic bits and pieces and a silver bell. All are thrown into a plastic basket in front of him on the settee, and with much encouragement and a little help, Luke removes them one by one.

Sally praises him enthusiastically throughout – all part of the reinforcement, or reward, principle. As well as persuading him to pick up the objects, she's checking that he is opening his hands, which tend to be closed, and following his own movements with his eyes. She then helps Luke's mother, Catherine, with his crawling exercises, prescribed by a physiotherapist. Then it's time to get out Luke's chart, which has to be filled in regularly, and to demonstrate next week's goal.

The 90-minute visit is relaxed and informal. Catherine says that starting to work with Luke has taken a load off her mind:

'I've known for months that Luke had problems but nobody would take any notice. We have a little girl, now 2 years old, who was a very early developer and friends would laugh and say I couldn't expect Luke to be like her. They'd say boys are lazier and second children don't talk as early as the first or it's because he's chubby. You want to believe it, but I knew it was more.

Finally the health visitor referred Luke to a paediatrician. She couldn't say exactly what was wrong so it's a case of wait and see for the moment. I was getting really desperate though, feeling I should be helping him in some way and not knowing how to. You feel so helpless. Then I read about Portage in a booklet on services for the under-5s, and I asked to be referred.

It's great to be able to work at home with him and have Sally come in rather than have to go out. I was offered the chance to attend a child development centre, but I turned it down for the moment. It's nice to be able to meet other mums whose children are going well, but I was afraid there would be lots of children there who were severely handicapped and it would make me depressed, wondering if Luke was going to turn out like that.

Luke's already making progress. In the last two weeks he's started sitting up and opening out his hands. He's also much more interested in everything going on around him. I just feel that much better knowing I'm doing everything I can to help him.'

SPEAKING FOR THEMSELVES

BRIONY

With a welcoming smile, Briony reaches out a plump little hand to touch you. She sits on the cosily-carpeted floor playing happily with her toys. She hardly ever cries. Her mother, Jane, says she is the perfect baby. Briony is 13 months old and has Down's Syndrome and a serious heart condition. Jane and her husband, Steve, both in their thirties, live in a detached house on a modern estate on the edge of a town. Both work, commuting to a nearby city; she is a music librarian, he is a printer. They have another child, 5-year-old Lucy.

Steve: 'They didn't tell us immediately after she was born. They waited till we were virtually walking out the hospital door, taking her home.'

Jane: 'Looking back now I don't understand why I didn't spot the signals that something was wrong. Immediately she was born, on the

Thursday morning, she was whipped away and I was told the doctor was looking her over. When I was given a single room, I just thought I was lucky. Then when Briony was a day old, I was bathing her and a nurse came in and took her away again – to do some tests, she said. Still no warning bells rang.

'I'd had a Caesarean with Lucy, so Briony was my first normal birth. I thought maybe this was routine when you produced a baby the normal way. I never noticed anything different about the way she looked. Neither did the friends and relatives who visited. Afterwards, when they knew, only one person said she'd been suspicious, but she decided she was just imagining it.

'On the Monday evening, when I was due to go home, the doctor waited for Steve to arrive and then called us into his office. He said he'd been waiting for the result of some blood tests and started talking about chromosomes. Then we knew immediately. Steve has a cousin in her 30s with Down's, so we knew a bit about the condition.

'The doctor told us there were more test results to come through but he was 99 per cent certain. I think we went into shock; a numbness comes over you. There was the feeling that nobody knew quite what to say to us and that they wanted us out of the hospital as quickly as possible. They weren't unkind or anything – it was just the feeling that everyone would be more comfortable when we left.'

Steve: 'For the first week we were in a bit of a state. Jane would wander off, I'd go looking for her and find her standing in the middle of a room, crying. Or she'd find me in the same state. It was hard telling the relatives. My mum and dad were shattered. Jane's dad took it in his stride. He came round straight away, took one look at her and said she was a beautiful baby and it didn't matter a bit.'

Jane: 'I tried to phone people to break the news, but a friend I hadn't got through to arrived on the doorstep the day after we got home, saying, "Where's the beautiful baby, then?" I immediately burst into tears. I told one neighbour and she offered to tell the others. On the whole people were marvellous and natural about it. There were none of those embarrassed looks and people crossing the road to avoid you that I know has happened to other people. In fact people approached me because of her handicap. Indirectly Briony has brought more friendship and love into my life than I could have imagined.

'But it still hurt badly in the early days. One of my worst experiences was standing at the window watching the normal kids going off to school. They all looked so unrealistically perfect to me and all I could think was that Briony would never be like that. Perhaps it's fortunate I go to work. If I was at home and meeting other mothers and toddlers I'd be comparing her all the time and feeling very sorry for myself. As it is, she's the only baby I know and she's lovely.

'I think the only negative reaction I've had was from an acquaintance who asked if I was going to keep her. As if she came with a guarantee and could be returned as faulty. I've learned since that it wasn't as ridiculous a remark as it sounded. Of five babies born with Down's Syndrome at a hospital in this area, three were left there for fostering or adoption. That particular hospital apparently takes a very negative view of handicapped children and offers parents the option of leaving them. Looking at Briony now and thinking of the pleasure she gives us, I feel sorry for those parents.'

Steve: 'I think having a member of the family with Down's already helped us come to terms with Briony. Sue, my cousin, is a great girl. She lives in a group home, has a boyfriend, goes to college and is fairly capable of looking after herself. We'll be very happy if our daughter turns out that well.'

Jane: 'We're not going to push her beyond her capabilities, but if she can cope, I would like her to go to mainstream school. I want her to live in the community, not tucked away in some backwater, and lead as normal a life as possible. I don't expect to have her at home for ever. Normal children leave the nest when they grow up, so why shouldn't those with a handicap?

'I'm quite selfish and not the maternal type. I couldn't devote my life to looking after one child. I've seen parents who do that and they look old and worn before their time. Briony has to fit in with our life. She's no more and no less important than any other member of the family.

'We'd like another child, partly for Lucy's sake. She's never shown any jealousy of her little sister and she enjoys playing with her, but having a sister with a handicap can be a burden. It would be nice for her to have a brother or sister to share it. They've told us that we run no higher risk than average of having another Down's child. They say Steve having a cousin with the condition is just coincidence. But I don't know. I've met too many people with a Down's child who have another Down's relative somewhere in the family not to make me suspicious.

'By the time we'd be having another baby, I'd be in my late thirties. I used to think I'd be tested and have a termination if there was a problem, but after Briony I no longer feel that Down's Syndrome is a justifiable reason for an abortion. So we'd probably go ahead and take pot luck. We don't want another like Briony, but if it happened it wouldn't be the end of the world.

'I was annoyed that the hospital where she was born took several days to tell us about her condition, but I was told later that this is their policy. They like to give you a few days to bond with the baby. I now believe they are right. Say we were told immediately after the birth, before we'd seen her, and then given the option of having her fostered. We might just have accepted. It doesn't bear thinking about.

'We've been very lucky in meeting professionals who take a positive attitude and stress the things Briony can do instead of the problems. She sat up at 7 months, just a month later than Lucy, and she's always played really well with her toys. I know she'll be slower; I accept that. She doesn't always understand what we're trying to get across. For instance, she thinks "No" is the funniest word in the world. She gets hysterical when I use it to her.

'I went back to work a couple of months after she was born. I've always felt very, very strongly about working and there was no question of me not going back, as I had after Lucy. The fact that she's a Down's baby didn't change that. They were happy to have her at the private nursery Lucy used to go to. She fits in beautifully; they love her. She's such an easy baby, always sweet-tempered and no sleep problems.'

Steve: 'And we do know what we're talking about. Lucy was the most difficult baby imaginable for the first year. Once she could walk, she started to improve, but until then she never seemed to sleep and she cried and cried.'

Jane: 'It nearly split us up. I remember Steve flinging a feeding bottle against a door and storming out, shouting, "Either she goes or I go." With Briony the initial shock, and then the second shock of discovering she had a heart condition, brought us closer, if anything.

'Briony had an emergency operation at 11 weeks to correct two holes in her heart. It was terrifying. I'd read that only 40 per cent of babies survive it, but our Briony's tough.'

Throughout the interview Steve fed and played with Briony. Jane says he genuinely does share the care. Because of shift work, he is the one who is there on the one day a week the Portage teacher comes. He looks after her if Jane needs to go out, but generally they have no problem finding babysitters so that they can go out together.

Jane: 'The grandparents are quite happy to have her and we are members of the neighbourhood babysitting circle. Circle members were a bit wary of looking after her at first, mainly because of her heart condition, but after one sit they stopped worrying.'

Steve: 'I enjoy having her, but it's not something I talk to the lads at work about. Some of them know but they don't show much interest. But then men don't talk about their normal kids much either.'

Jane: 'I think there's a particular stigma for a man in having a child who's less than perfect. It's a sort of reflection on his masculinity – or at least men think it is. It seems to be easier for a man to accept a daughter with a handicap though. A girl is allowed to be weaker.

'Maybe people who don't have a child with a handicap will always think those who have are a little bit . . . I don't know how you'd put it . . . odd. We didn't join the Down's Children's Association for a while, partly because we had a funny idea of what the other parents in it were like. We thought they wouldn't be "like us", but when we started meeting them, they were perfectly ordinary people, some like us, some not. They go right across the social spectrum.

'I read every book I can lay my hands on about other families' experiences. The one I read that really stuck in my mind was by a mother who compared having a Down's child to booking a holiday in Italy and when you step off the plane finding you are actually in Holland. At first you protest because you wanted the sun and the sea and the sand, but gradually you find that Holland has a lot going for it too. It has windmills and a slower pace and another kind of pleasure. It wasn't what you planned for or wanted, but you find you like it anyway. That's Briony, you see – our little Dutch windmill!'

PETER

Born prematurely by Caesarean section, Peter weighed only 4 pounds and spent a month in a premature baby unit. There was no suggestion that there would be further problems, but from the moment he came home he was, in his mother, Anne's, words, 'a very, very unsettled baby, always screaming.' It's a familiar story. 'I couldn't get anyone to take me seriously, even when Jim and I were having to look after him in shifts so that we could each get a bit of sleep. The clinic said it was colic and our doctor said it was usually ears or stomach with small babies and gave me something for both.'

Finally, at a routine hospital appointment, it was acknowledged that there was something 'seriously wrong'. He was treated for spasms, ('He started smiling once he was no longer in pain,' Anne says. 'It was wonderful to see.') and they were referred to a consultant.

Peter is now 2½ and has cerebral palsy. He lies on the floor chuckling, while his 6-year-old sister, Amy, hugs and tickles him. He is a happy little boy, but as dependent as a baby. His father, Jim, is an engineer who often works from home.

Anne: 'I took Peter to see the consultant on my own, which was a mistake. He was a very busy man. There was no time for breaking the news gently. It was a case of, "Your baby has serious brain damage, next please." I was just turned out into the hospital corridor with this information going round in my head. I rang Jim to come and get me and I stood there sobbing, holding Peter, while people hurried by. Eventually a kind nursing officer stopped and asked me what was wrong. She took me somewhere quiet and stayed with me till Jim came.'

Jim: 'Of course it was devastating. We knew something was wrong but you don't quite believe it till it's confirmed. I felt angry with everyone, particularly the consultant, who asked Anne why we hadn't taken Peter to the doctor sooner. We'd taken him everywhere. I was angry too about all the people who hadn't helped. And I felt a bit guilty. Maybe if we'd tried harder, banged our heads against more brick walls, something could have been done earlier.'

Anne: 'For me it was like my baby had died. The little boy I'd imagined Peter would grow up to be had gone. It was made worse by the consultant saying he'd be blind (which wasn't true) and severely retarded; practically a vegetable.

'During the gaps between hospital appointments, I'd begin to see that he had a personality of his own and could enjoy life in a limited fashion, but I'd go back to the hospital and they'd tell me something awful and send me out in tears again. I was on a see-saw. I'd just have time to pick myself up and then I'd be slapped down again.

'The turning point for me came when Amy said to me, "I'm fed up with you crying." It shocked me into thinking about her and Jim. Life goes on and you've got to make the best of what it throws at you. It also helped that by then, Peter was becoming a real little person. I decided to believe the evidence of my own eyes rather than what the hospital said. The hospital only saw the handicap, I saw the little boy underneath.'

Jim: 'The best bit of advice we had was from the health visitor who told us, "Peter lives with you, you don't live with Peter." Peter has to take his place in the family. The world doesn't have to revolve around him.'

Anne: 'She was wonderful, our health visitor. She made me realize I shouldn't run myself into the ground trying to do everything for Peter, or the rest of the family would suffer. I didn't want to upset Jim and Amy or my parents by crying in front of them, but I could cry with her.

'We had a visiting teacher before Peter started school – he goes two days a week – and she was good too. It was she who accidentally told me what Peter's condition was. "These kids with cerebral palsy . . ." she began one day, and I thought, "So that's what he's got." Nobody had actually given him a label before. I went out and bought all the books on the subject I could find, and I began to understand Peter much better.

'Before he started school, I used to take him to a group for handicapped children at the hospital, where a speech therapist told me I should put my lips against his and say words. I did this half-heartedly, not expecting anything back and almost at once he began saying "Mum Mum". He'll say words that appeal to him. As for being blind, he has sight deficiencies, but if you hold a bar of chocolate in front of him, he sees it quickly enough!

'His school is good. It's got a swimming pool, medical staff. There's someone who comes in from a nearby school for the blind to do visual stimulation with children like Peter. My only niggle is that I don't seem to be as involved as I want to be. I asked the physiotherapist if she could teach me some exercises to do at home with Peter, and she said I wasn't to worry about it; it was their job. But I want to help.'

A social worker suggested that the family could benefit from a break and put them in touch with another family who would look after Peter for a few hours or a weekend.

Anne: 'The idea is that you get so many hours paid for by social services and it's up to you to book the times you want with the host family. It's a good idea but somehow it hasn't worked for us. The first woman we met was nice, but she was right on the other side of town, and had a lot of children of her own. Peter wouldn't settle with all that noise and coming and going.

'Then we were introduced to someone nearer to us. She was lovely but she has young children and I find it difficult to ring her and ask her to have Peter when she's so busy, even though I know she gets paid. I don't know what it is. Maybe you don't have long enough time to get to know the host family. I'd need to have known them for months, like friends, before I'd feel happy. It's okay at the moment; the two days at school give me a breather, and soon he'll be going for five days. But we'll need breaks in the school holidays to take Amy out. I don't want her to suffer.'

Jim worries that they might not be doing enough for Peter. Friends suggest taking him to the Peto clinic in Hungary, 'or any new cure they read about in the papers'.

Jim: 'There's no evidence any of them would work for Peter and there isn't the time or the money to try everything. I am sure whatever we try we'll end up, when he's older, saying we should have tried the other. He's a happy child, despite his problems. I see lots of able-bodied kids who aren't as happy. Peter enjoys things. He loves splashing about in water, playing with his sister. He loves the dog and chocolate.

'I think a lot about the future. I want to start a trust fund so that there will be money there for him if we die. It sounds morbid but you have to think of everything.

'It's amazed me how many people I meet now who have a handicapped child or a friend or relative who has. I wait for people to mention it first. I don't bring Peter into coversations normally, because the attitude to you can change subtly. It's as if they start feeling sorry for you. I'm not ashamed of my son. In fact I'm proud of him; he's a smashing little kid.'

Anne: 'Not that you want a handicapped child. Nobody does. You make the best of it and you find there are good things as well as bad. What really annoys me though is when people say, "I don't know how you cope, I couldn't have . . ." As if you had a choice!'

MARK

Mark is 4 years old and a real livewire. He tears around the family's small living room, demanding a drink, toys, someone to play with. He shouts loud enough to drown out normal conversation and when asked gently by his mother to be a little quieter, points out indignantly that he is singing! His speech is impossible for a stranger to understand but the indignation needs no translation.

Mark has Down's Syndrome. His parents, Sally and David, have one other child, 11-year-old James. David works for a Christian organization and both stress that being committed Christians influenced their attitude to Mark's birth.

David: 'We were told that Mark had special needs a few hours after his birth. It was handled as well as such things can be. The curtains were drawn around the bed and a doctor told us together. He explained that a consultant paediatrician would call to see us at home to talk to us and answer queries – and this happened a few days after Sally and Mark came home from hospital.

'There is no painless way to break the news. It was devastating, a major shock, but we were glad to know straight away because it enabled us to make certain decisions within a day of the birth. We agreed that we would always be open with one another and never hide what we felt; that we'd never play on people's sympathy (we don't want anyone saying, "Poor you, you've got a child with special needs") and that we would never use Mark for financial gain. Bleeding the system would not cure the pain in us. We accept welfare benefits but only those that we fairly deserve. For instance, we were initially given day and night attendance allowance, but when we found that Mark was sleeping at night and didn't require more attention than any normal young child, we chose to give up the night-time portion. It caused tremendous administrative problems. Nobody seemed to know what to do about it. Apparently it doesn't happen often.

'Perhaps most importantly, we promised to accept Mark for who he was, to accept this child as a gift from God.'

Sally: 'Acceptance isn't easy. You first have to relinquish all the dreams and aspirations you had during pregnancy. I never thought it mattered to me that my child should take GCSE and A-levels, but when Mark was born and I knew that he's never to do these things, I was forced to acknowledge that they did matter to me. I had to re-evaluate what was important in life. And it *is* more important for your child to be a happy, loving person than that he passes exams.

'I went through all the well-documented stages. The grieving for the child you've lost, the numbness, the anger. I'm sometimes asked to talk as a parent to professionals and I tell them not to take it personally if a mother or father rants and raves at them. The anger really isn't directed at them as individuals. A lot of parents have feelings of guilt – was it something I did or failed to do? At least when you have a child with a known genetic condition, like Mark, you know it happened at conception and there was nothing you could do.

'I think everyone goes through mood swings and depression when they find out their child has a handicap, whether the diagnosis is made at birth or a couple of years later. You dwell on the negative things; the future looks so bleak. Our best bit of advice came from the paediatrician who told us to try and live one day at a time. You simply don't know what will happen in ten years' time, so it's pointless worrying about it.

'The hardest part of Mark's handicap for me has been the lack of communication. Though he can understand a lot, he can't tell us how he feels. We have to try and guess what is bothering him. It's upsetting for us and terribly frustrating for him when we can't understand.

'It's probably a good thing that there is a gap between him and his brother. I'd forgotten exactly what James did at different stages and couldn't keep comparing them. But I did compare him with other normal children his age. I found it very hard to be around playgrounds and places where you could see children of Mark's age doing all the things he couldn't do. I still find it hard, but I force myself to take him to such places where he can mix with ordinary children. They stimulate him, and in a small way he's breaking down barriers. Hopefully, if able children get to know and understand those with handicaps, they'll grow up more tolerant and enlightened adults. A lot of adults as well as children have a fear of people with a mental handicap, but that's because they don't know what to expect.'

David and Sally had some experience of Down's Syndrome before Mark was born. They lived for a time in a religious community where a Down's man, living with his mother, was one of the other residents.

Sally: 'It helped us to know what to expect and it helped when we had to tell James about his baby brother. But it wasn't enough to stop him being disappointed and very, very upset. At first he didn't tell anyone at school, though, in fact, once they knew all his school friends were fantastic with Mark. They always come to say hello to him and he loves the attention.

'My family accepted immediately but David's found it harder. His father has a twin brother who was in a mental home and was never spoken about. That coloured his attitude. David's mother simply doesn't accept there is anything wrong. She'll say: "He'll be alright when he grows up." I say, gently, "Actually, Mum, he won't but we love him as he is." It doesn't seem to make any difference; she's convinced.

'There's no lack of acceptance or shortage of babysitters from the people we meet through our work. In Mark's first six months of life he came with us to Spain and Africa. It helped somehow being surrounded by people.

'As a mother, you don't get the chance not to accept your child. You are with him all the time. I think it's harder for men. Having a special needs child seems to hurt their manly pride. Some of them deliberately distance themselves so that they won't feel the hurt and disappointment too keenly.'

David: 'I think there's also the feeling that they can't pile their grief on to their wife who is already suffering, so they pretend it doesn't exist. This is why we made a point of always being open with each other. There is always pain in your heart and it would be easy to become hard, to harden yourself against the pain, but it's important to let yourself feel it.'

Mark attends an ordinary day nursery part-time and has access to a short-stay unit run by Social Services.

Sally: 'Where we lived before there was hardly anything for families. Even on the other side of this city there's not much, but for some reason, on this side, there are so many alternatives it's hard to choose. We don't use the respite unit much for overnight stays, but we often leave Mark there for a day if we want to go out together.

'The nursery, which is for normal children but welcomes those with special needs, has a speech therapist and physiotherapist who see Mark. We also have a visiting teacher to work with him at home once a fortnight. When he was younger, we had a Portage worker, but though she never put pressure on me, I used to feel guilty if I hadn't worked with Mark every day. You have certain goals to achieve and charts to fill in and for me it added to the burden. The visiting teacher service is less rigid, though we won't need it for much longer because Mark is starting school next term.

'We make a point of not dwelling on the future, but occasionally you have to think about practical issues. Will Mark stay at home with us always – or would he, later, be happier and more stimulated living away from home? Our views fluctuate. If he were to live elsewhere we'd like it to be in a Christian community, like Acorn, an organization which runs homes and links in with churches.

'But I don't know if I'd ever be able to come to terms with him leaving. When he stayed for a night in the respite unit, I had a real sense of guilt. I feel guilty just thinking about the possibility of sending him away.'

JASON

Sharon lives with her son, Jason, in a pleasant ground-floor maisonette on a large council estate. It's the area where she grew up, and her parents and two married sisters live nearby. She sees her boyfriend, the father of her son, regularly, but they have no plans to marry.

Jason, aged 2½, was born when she was 16. Sharon says she only realized she was pregnant shortly before the birth. Her parents didn't know until she went into labour.

Jason, a sturdy-looking little boy despite his mental and physical handicaps, lies on his back on the floor, sucking his dummy and playing with the toys which hang above him. After a while, he begins to rock his head from side to side and soon falls asleep.

Sharon: 'He'll sleep there till I try to put him to bed, then he'll be awake half the night. He's terrible at night. He wears me out. I hardly get a wink of sleep. He goes to a short stay unit every Wednesday and Thursday night – my social worker fixed that up – and my mum has him Friday nights. Otherwise, I don't think I could manage. Mum didn't believe how bad he was at night till I stayed with her for a week, between moving from my last place to here. She thought I was putting it on. When she saw I wasn't she said she'd look after him one night a week. It gives me the chance to go out.

'My family love Jason. If he's not been well, my sisters and mum and dad are on the phone asking how he is. And he loves them too. He gets all excited when he hears my dad's voice, and when my sister's kids come round, he sits in his chair and giggles and shakes all over with excitement. They laugh at him and that sends him into even more fits of giggles.

'When I'm here on my own with him though, it's a different story. He gets bored and cries. He goes on and on. Every time I walk across the room he'll start crying and he won't stop till I pick him up. It's not that he wants to be cuddled. He hates being held tight. He just wants to lie across my lap and wave his hands about.

'It drives me mad, the crying. There have been times when I've just had to put him in his bedroom, close the door and let him have his little tantrum. Sometimes I think I can't carry on a day longer.

'Now he's started school it's a bit better, though I don't like the way he gets picked up by the bus at eight in the morning and doesn't get home till five. They have to pick up from a wide area, you see. By the time he gets here, he's so exhausted he falls asleep immediately and then, of course, he's awake all night.

'I wouldn't want to move nearer the school though. After he was born they put me in a multi-storey block, miles from here. I hated it. I knew no one, the lifts didn't work half the time, so I used to have to carry Jason and the pushchair up flights of stairs.

'There are no stairs here and I can see my family. During the week I look after my little niece while my sister is out at work. She's just 7 weeks younger than Jason. When he's here she's all over him, playing with him. She's no burden. Having her here takes some of the pressure to entertain Jason off me.'

Jason was premature and spent 10 days in a special baby unit.

Sharon: 'You couldn't see anything wrong with him at first. He seemed a normal little baby. He still looks normal. But having my sister's little girl around showed up the problems. She was doing all these clever things, and Jason was doing nothing.

'My mum used to say, "Take him to the hospital, find out what's going on." When I did, they said they couldn't find anything wrong, but I took him back again and they finally admitted that he was handicapped. Even then they couldn't tell me what exactly was wrong with him. He hasn't got cerebral palsy, he hasn't got all sorts of things, but they don't seem to know what he has got.

'A little while ago, they took pictures of him and made notes about how small his feet are and how he has little dimples in his knees. They say all these signs mean that he may have a very rare condition. I get really upset when they can't tell me what he's got. If I knew, maybe I could talk to other mothers who've got children with the same condition. They could give me some advice and encourage me.

'I don't like the specialist I take him to anyway. I've just written to her saying I want to change to someone else. She never talks to me. I go into her room and it's full of people – students, I suppose, nobody tells me. I just sit there with Jason and she ignores me and talks to them about my son. I might as well not be there. It's so insulting, and I can't even understand what she's saying because it's all in doctor language. I want a doctor who treats me as a normal, sensible person and talks to me, not over my head.

'My social worker is okay. I get on well with her. She's young and I feel we're on the same wavelength. She tells me to apply for anything that's going. I've had a washing machine off the Family Fund, and I've applied for the cost of a holiday for me and Jason and mum and dad. I need to take my parents to help. The next thing I'm going to ask for is the cost of driving lessons. I should get mobility allowance for Jason when he is five, and then I'll be able to get a car and take him out. He hates travelling by bus.'

Recently Jason has had stomach problems, which have been diagnosed as an allergy to certain foods. For two months, he's been taken off white bread and dairy produce, among other things. Her doctor advised Sharon to substitute soya for cow's milk, but, she says, no other substitutes were suggested and she was surprised to hear of the existence of soya and vegetable margarines.

Sharon: 'No one said. I've been trying to get him to eat dry brown bread. My mum makes him milky puddings with soya milk but it's not the same; he doesn't like it. It's been really hard keeping him on the diet. I hope they'll say he can go back on ordinary food soon.

'It's all hard, really. School has helped. They've got him holding a spoon, which is the first step to feeding himself. But he's still in nappies and can't sit up on his own. I don't think I've accepted that he'll always be like this. I still hope that one day he'll walk and talk. Every day I wake up thinking, "Maybe today he'll do something amazing." I know for sure that if he's this handicapped when he's older I won't be able to look after him. I've told my parents and they don't like it but they'll have to accept it. I just couldn't cope.'

SARA

Sara is severely handicapped, mentally and physically, by a rare genetic condition. Although only two, she has recently started school. Her mother, Nicki, works as a medical secretary. Her father is a doctor. They have one other child, 4-year-old Tim.

Nicki: 'I knew there was something wrong from the start but it took me such a long time to get the medical profession to take me seriously, including my husband. She wouldn't breast-feed so I changed her to the bottle. It used to take me 2 hours to feed her and then she'd vomit it all back and I'd have to start again.

'I kept telling people at the clinic, at the hospital, but she was never sick in front of them so they'd just fob me off. It's funny, their attitude. It's not as if they disbelieve you exactly, but they can't quite accept what you are saying till they see it with their own two eyes. They'd say it was nothing to worry about, and I'd come away desperate because I knew it was.

'Sara was finally admitted to hospital at 9 weeks old because she wasn't gaining weight. If they hadn't taken her in, I think I would have had a nervous breakdown. Those nine weeks were hardest of my life. I was trying to look after a sick baby, I had a lively toddler, and I was on my own most of the time. My husband works such long hours he is hardly ever home, my mother has a full-time job, so it was just me. I was tired, depressed, confused and desperate for sleep.

'When I went to visit Sara in hospital, a nurse said, "She's been sick. We see what you mean." It was such a relief. Someone else knew and could share the burden. I got the first good night's sleep I'd had since she was born.

'They gave her all sorts of tests, the poor little mite. No wonder she's so nervous now. I suppose at the back of my mind, I thought it would turn out to be something treatable. My husband did too. He's a very quiet man. He doesn't show his feelings and he'll never make a fuss or interfere at the hospital. He's had other doctors interfere when he's been treating their family and he knows how embarrassing and annoying it can be. In a way his profession is a disadvantage. In other ways it's an advantage because people are more straight with us.

'As it turned out it was bad news. Her condition is so rare that nobody can give us a prognosis. Will she improve or get worse? What will her lifespan be? Nobody knows. At the moment she's tiny and frail and very nervous. She has to be fed by naso-gastric tube. I have no idea what she'll be like in a couple of years' time. On a bad day I see myself in middle age still tied down with an adult infant.

'My husband says I shouldn't worry; if necessary we can employ someone to help look after her. But that's not the point. Maybe you come to terms with it gradually. When she was six months old, I couldn't see myself still coping when she was 2 or 3. Now I can't imagine it being like this when she's 5.'

Nicki went back to her hospital job as a medical secretary a year ago.

Nicki: 'It was go to work or go round the bend. I was getting very lonely and depressed. Work is my lifeline. I'm too busy there to think about my own problems. Physically I'm shattered, but mentally I'm much better.

'I hit a very low point when the hospital, after diagnosing Sara, made it clear there was no more they could do and referred me to a group for children with handicaps at a child development centre. I didn't want to go there. It meant admitting I had a handicapped child and I didn't want to be part of the whole handicap thing.

'I said I'd think it over, not planning to turn up, but someone from the centre arrived and persuaded me to go. I hardly dared look at the other children the first time, I was so scared of what I might see. I felt drained when I got home, but I was glad I'd gone. There were all kinds of specialists there, under one roof, and place for the normal kids to play, too. And none of the other mums stared or asked me what was wrong with Sara, which was such a relief after the looks you get from the public at large.

'The reaction of the public has been one of the hardest things to bear. Maybe I'm hyper-sensitive. People stare openly at Sara. Given half a chance they come up and ask you questions about the feeding tube in her nose and personal things I don't want to discuss with complete strangers.

'It was the same when she was in hospital for tests. The other mothers would gather round and ask me questions. It was like the Spanish Inquisition. I came home and said to my husband, "That's it. I'm not visiting her again. You can go." He persuaded me I didn't have to involve myself with the other mothers if I didn't want to. I could sit by Sara and turn my back. In the end that's how I handled it. I'm sure they thought me very peculiar, but so what!

'Tim, my 4 year old, was very jealous of her at first. I'm sure he thought he'd got rid of her when she went into hospital, but she came back. I don't think he's twigged she's different yet; he's too young to understand. The other day I heard him call her "My Sara", which must be a good sign! I'm sure it will affect him later, but I can't begin to think that far ahead. It only depresses me.'

Sara spends three out of every four weekends at a Social Services unit near home. When Nicki went back to work, the private nursery Tim attended took her daughter as well and she employed someone to pick them up and look after them till she returned in the evening. The same woman is there now to meet the minibus which takes Sara to and from school.

Nicki: 'It was heartbreaking to send her off to school on the bus the first few weeks. She's such a tiny little dot, no bigger than a baby. I mean, you don't even send an able bodied 5 year old to school alone, you take them yourself.

'It's a large, very well equipped school which takes children with a variety of handicaps and has physiotherapists and speech therapists, and its own pool. She's much more interested in what's happening around her since she's been there. I think she understands a lot. When I pick her out of her cot in the morning, she's peering about with these bright brown eyes, taking everything in.

'Her tiniest little achievement is something to get excited about. When she kissed her teddy bear the other day, I wept. I got on the phone to my mother straight away to tell her. When I think of the things Tim was doing at her age and how I took them for granted. . . .

'I adore Sara – everyone in the family does – but I have strong views about handicapped children and the family, views I know a lot of people don't agree with. I believe that the three of us, outside of Sara, who make up the family unit, are ultimately more important. If having Sara at home was harming us, as a family, then I would consider sending her into residential care.'

DEBBIE

It's a house full of children (Julie and Alan have five), chat and family clutter. In the midst of it all, 4-year-old Debbie sits on a settee, making popping noises with her mouth – blowing kisses, her mother calls it – and gazes at you with brown, button eyes. She is not yet toilet-trained, says a few words, like 'Hello' and 'Bye' when coaxed and makes a valiant attempt at walking when an adult holds her hands. The medical diagnosis is that she is microcephalic.

Julie: 'But I find that hard to believe. It means she has a small head and she hasn't, not in proportion to her little body. I still think she was damaged at birth by lack of oxygen. She was severely asphyxiated, and though she was a big baby, 8lbs 4ozs., she was in the special baby unit.

'I wasn't worried at first, but as they were preparing to take me to the open ward, a sister spoke to the nurse and I was put in a room of my own. I knew then that something was up. I'd been through this business before and if they give you a single room, there's a reason.

'After a bit, the doctor came to see me and said the baby had problems and mightn't live. There was no mention of any particular condition. I said, "You mean she's been damaged?" It just seemed to be assumed that it was the lack of oxygen that had damaged her brain.

'I felt very low after the birth anyway and just couldn't stop crying. I told Alan when he came in and, well, he was just in shock really. But Debbie rallied and when I left hospital a week later she was well enough to come home. She was just like any other baby at first, no problem.

'I used to take her to the child development centre at the hospital and there were physios and social workers there. They always seemed to be telling me she was slow or she wasn't doing this or that when she should be. It was very depressing. But some people there were helpful. There was a social worker who explained about a nursery run by a voluntary group that Debbie could go to if we wanted. She didn't push me. She just said, "When you're ready." Debbie started at the nursery when she was 2. They used to pick her up in a minibus. She went to school at 3.

'She's not a difficult child, though she had a spell when, if I took her out shopping and stopped for a coffee, she'd just scream and scream. Mostly she fits in with the family. We've just been on holiday and she did most of the things the other kids did, only I had to be with her, of course. She couldn't even paddle on her own. It's at times like that it hits you that she's different. Coming up to 5, the others could do so much.

'Having the other children around is good for her. She's never lonely or bored. She can't talk to them, but I think she takes in a lot. It's hard to be sure, but she's very alert. Sometimes I worry I'm not doing enough for her. You hear about methods of treatment that are supposed to work wonders like conductive education or patterning, and you think, "If I did that she might really improve."

'We went down to the Institute for Brain Injured Children to see the work they do there, patterning children. But you have to work almost the whole day, every day, with the child, and have lots of people in to help with the exercises. I didn't see how we could do it, not with the other kids. It wouldn't be fair if I spent all my time with one. But then you think, "Is it fair to her if I don't do it?" You feel torn.

'The school is good. Even during the holidays the physiotherapist pops in to see how she is and to give me some exercises to do with her. But they've got a lot of kids to see to, not just mine. There isn't much time for individual attention at school and if you don't push Debbie really hard she won't do anything. There's always this nagging feeling that you, or someone, should be doing more.

'The paediatrician at the hospital — we take Debbie to see her about every five months — didn't discourage us from trying different treatments, but she did say that she doesn't think it necessary because Debbie will get there anyway. They say she's got a lot going for her. It's just a case of waiting for it all to come together — and no one can tell me when that will happen.

'I've never said much to the other kids about what is wrong with Debbie. I did try with my 11-year old once. I started to say, "Your sister is handicapped . . .", and she said, "Oh, I know all that." They seem to just accept the way she is. If they bring friends home, the only thing the friends want to know is why she can't walk. I say, "She will, she's just a bit slower at doing things."

'I don't use the term "mentally handicapped" because I associate it with mad people. People use mental to mean mad don't they? I always say "learning difficulties". It's the same with the word "fits": Debbie does have small fits, but to the kids I call them her "jumps". It's less frightening.

'I probably sound as if we haven't any problems, but there are days when I get really depressed, when the way Debbie is seems a tragedy, a waste. I've got to carry on because of the others. One of the things that gets to me is that I don't know why she's like this. I had four healthy children and I carried her for 9 months with no problem. What went wrong?

'Alan know how low I get and he tries not to bring the subject up. He doesn't talk about Debbie anyway, though I know he loves her like the others. To be honest, I haven't a clue how he feels about her or about the future. We never talk about it. I suppose he thinks if you can't change it, why talk about it.

'But you can change some things. I set myself little goals. I've set my heart on her walking now. We're always getting her up on her feet. There are so many things she could do and see if she was walking. I can't bear to think of her in a wheelchair with all the restrictions. When I look ahead, that's about the worst thing I can imagine.'

GETTING HELP

Attendance Allowance
Tax-free allowance for children and adults who are severely disabled and need frequent help with bodily functions and/or continual supervision, during the day and/or night. Paid at two rates: (a) lower rate for someone who needs attention day *or* night, and (b) higher rate for someone needing attention day and night. Available from 6 months old if there is proof that the child needs substantially more attention than a normal baby of the same age.

Claim on form NI 20, available from any DSS office or from the

Attendance Allowance Unit,
DSS,
North Fylde Central Office,
Norcross,
Blackpool FY5 ETA.

When Attendance and Mobility Allowances combine to form one allowance, the Disability Living Allowance, there will be a third, lower rate of Attendance Allowance available to some people who don't qualify for the higher rates.

Contact-a-Family
A national charity which has links with over 700 independent self-help/mutual support groups throughout Britain. Offers support

and advice to parents or professionals wishing to start a group in their neighbourhood.

Contact-a-Family,
16 Strutton Ground,
London SW1P 2HP.
Tel: 071 222 2695.

Disabled Living Foundation

Provides information on all aspects of living with disability, including equipment and technical aids, clothing and footwear, incontinence, services and benefits.

Disabled Living Foundation,
380–384 Harrow Road,
London W9 2HU.
Tel: 071 289 6111.

Disabled Living Centres

Permanent displays of equipment which can be inspected and tried out. Over 30 Centres around Britain. Their addresses are available from:

Disabled Living Centres Council,
76 Clarendon Park Road,
Leicester LE2 3AD.
Tel: 0533 70747/8.

Family Fund

Helps families caring for a child up to 16, with severe handicap, by suppling items not available through Health of Social Services. For example, they often provide washing machines, tumble dryers, bedding, equipment, holiday expenses, driving lessons. Not means-tested, but family circumstances may sometimes be taken into account.

The Family Fund,
P.O. Box 50,
York YO1 1UV.
Tel: 0904 21115.

Genetic Counselling

There are genetic counselling centres in most main cities. Ask your GP for a referral.

In Touch

Newsletter for families with a handicapped child, circulated to members in all parts of Britain. Very good at putting parents who have a child with a rare condition in touch with others.

Ann Worthington,
In Touch,
10 Norman Road,
Sale,
Cheshire M33 3DF.
Tel: 061 905 2440.

Invalid Care Allowance

This is intended for people who are unable to work because they care for a disabled person. The person you look after has to be getting Attendance Allowance and you must spend at least 35 hours a week caring for them. You are allowed to earn a small weekly amount before losing benefit.

ICA Unit,
Palatine House,
Lancaster Road,
Preston,
Lancs PR1 1NS.

National Toy Libraries Association

Addresses of local toy libraries.

68 Churchway,
London NW1 1LT
Tel: 071 833 0991.

Orange Badge Parking Scheme

Allows parking concessions for driver or passenger, aged 2 upwards, with a severe physical disability, which makes walking impossible or very difficult. Contact your local Social Services Department initially.

Portage

Home-based teaching scheme for pre-school children with special needs.

National Portage & Home Training Association,
Dept of Psychology,
University of Southampton,
Southampton SO9 5NH.

2 Schooldays

SCHOOL TODAY AND YESTERDAY

When my son started school, there was a near walk-out of teachers, all of whom refused to have a child so handicapped in their class. I only know this because the teacher who volunteered to take on a special care unit for Patrick and others like him has remained a friend.

This was 1972, when the 1971 Education Act had transferred responsibility for all special needs children to local authority education departments. Centres for children with mental handicap which had been able to pick and choose the children they catered for, were compelled to offer an education to the most profoundly handicapped and behaviourally difficult. They can't have found it easy at first.

I liked many things about the small 'neighbourhood' special school Patrick attended until he was eighteen; the headmistress, the staff, the fact that they knew me and I knew them and was involved in the life of the school, the way they accepted Patrick and his little idiosyncrasies – once they got over the initial shock. Less lovable was the shortage of facilities compared to larger special schools, the lack of space, and the way every child who did not fit productively into one of the other classes was tipped into the special care unit, so that the totally dependent and physically disabled were mixed with the hyperactive and aggressive.

But, as older parents will tell you, the often purpose-built schools of the 1970s were a vast improvement on what their children had to put up with – daily sessions held in draughty church halls, before the junior training centres, which metamorphosized into special schools, were built.

The schools of today have come a long way in a short time. No longer are they described as schools for the severely educationally subnormal (SSN or ESN (S)); they are now for children with severe learning difficulties (SLD). Even the smallest, for around forty children, are likely to have a steady stream of professionals – apart from teachers – visiting, including physiotherapists, speech therapists, paediatricians, opticians, dentists. It is less stressful for both parents and child to see a specialist on familiar territory than to endure a long wait in a crowded out-patients' department.

Children start school as young as 2 years old. Some schools take pupils from that age through to 19. Others cater for junior or senior age children only. A few offer sixth-form style units for over-16s, where the emphasis is on academic study and independence skills. Alternatively there is the opportunity for those who would benefit to go out to courses at colleges of further education, while keeping school as a base. Many people feel that since children with a mental handicap tend to develop at a slow but steady rate, it would be beneficial for some to carry on with education into their twenties.

One way in which school hasn't changed is that it is a very important place in the lives of both child and parents, particularly mothers who often get involved in parents' groups, and in helping out in a multitude of ways.

It's often the first place you meet other people with a handicapped child and problems like your own. If you are lucky, it is the place you can turn to for information and help, a gateway to other services. It's the place that not only stimulates and helps your child but offers you a daily break from caring. The long summer school holiday when all this stops is a nightmare to parents and bored child alike. Many schools now offer some form of playscheme for a few weeks. It helps, but what most parents would really like are longer school terms and shorter holidays. Teachers, not to mention their unions, blanch at the thought.

What kind of education can children expect in an SLD school? The school where Paul Thomas is headteacher is typical of many. The curriculum is different for each one of the 40 pupils, but they concentrate on five core areas – motor skills, social skills, cognition, self-help and communication, taking in, where possible, parts of the national curriculum.

Everything to be learned is broken down into small steps. Each child has an individual programme, which can only be carried out on a one-to-one basis, so each child has his or her share of time with teacher or classroom assistant. The children with severe multiple learning difficulties (Paul Thomas refuses to call them multi-handicapped or special care children) follow a modified programme. For example, while the more able are doing PE, they will have physiotherapy. As Paul Thomas says:

> Some of the children will learn to read at a simple level but it is important for them to have basic word recognition, learning terms such as "in", "out", "toilet", "danger", and functional numeracy like the number of the bus they get or their telephone number. The object is to make each child as independent as possible. Life is better for the children and easier for the families if they can use the toilet, wash themselves, make a cup of tea, travel on the bus.
>
> Everything that happens during the day is a teaching opportunity. At lunchtime the children are not just eating lunch or even learning to feed themselves. They are learning to make choices of what they want to eat – they all go up to the serving hatch, and if possible, indicate what they want to eat. They are learning anything from how to pour a drink to table manners and social interaction.
>
> All the children go out in the minibus. They go swimming, horse-riding, to the shops, the library, the park, a farm. The group with multiple learning difficulties have outings geared to them. Their swimming period takes place in a hydrotherapy pool belonging to another school. They recently had a special treat when staff from the Body Shop came in to give them aromatherapy.

Much of what is available in schools depends on the determination and interests of the head, the skills of the staff, and the generosity of the local education department. Hence one school I visited had installed conductive education equipment for children with physical as well as mental handicaps, and had a fascinating range of electronic toys – thanks to the special interest of one of the teachers. Another had a Snoezelen room for those with the most profound handicaps. This is a dark room filled with soft cushions and the stimulation of wall-to-wall sights, sounds and smells, including revolving mirror balls, fibre optics and bubble units.

If only they were all standard. Special schools have come a long way, it's true, but they still have some way to go.

SEGREGATION vs INTEGRATION

The hot special education issue of the moment is whether children with learning difficulties should be taught in their own specialized schools or integrated into mainstream schools, either in special units on the campus or side-by-side in the classroom with their non-handicapped peers.

There are thriving special units alongside ordinary schools, but relatively few children are being fully integrated at present, except for the very young in nursery or infant classes. The higher up the age level you go, the rarer it becomes, but in 1990 one girl with Down's Syndrome took her GCSE in a limited range of subjects alongside her peers, after progressing right through the mainstream school system. Others are following in her footsteps. The Down's Association is adamant that, given the chance, there are many more who could do equally well.

However optimistically you look at it though, only a small minority of children with learning difficulties are going to be exam successes; but there are other ways of integrating them. Springfield primary school in Derbyshire takes children with mental handicaps into its ordinary classrooms, 2, 3 or 4 to a class, with an extra teacher to help them.

They tackle the same subjects as their peers but on a different level. They are not expected to achieve the same standard but they stay with their own age group and will move on to secondary school with them. The headmaster is confident that this system helps the children with handicaps to improve and to socialize, and those without handicaps to understand and respect children less able than themselves – which is the main argument of the pro-integrationists.

Not all teachers are so convinced. In two special schools I visited I found two heads with very different views. Joyce Rowthorne, whose school is based amid much well-tended greenery in the grounds of a residential hospital, believes that 'all special schools should be shut down.' She feels that they cannot prepare children with learning difficulties for real, post-school life when they will not be isolated and protected.

Joyce Rowthorne's school, for children aged 2–19, is well equipped with computers and the lastest electronic toys, as well as Peto-style conductive education equipment, for children with multiple disabilities. Several children spend some time in a nearby mainstream secondary school and fit in well:

> They are having new experiences and they hold their own. Teachers often say about one of our children, "Hasn't he got beautiful table manners", meaning he is much better behaved at table than their normal children. I believe their kids are growing up accepting disability and that bodes well for the future generation. Able kids have a lot of natural sympathy. The biggest problem is not that they will tease or bully a child but that they all want to push the wheelchair or look after them. If anything they over-protect them.

Paul Thomas, whose school caters for forty 2–13 year olds, agrees with the last statement, but he sees it as one of many reasons why special schools should stay. His school, under a different education authority from Joyce Rowthorne's, is situated on a busy, rather run-down city street. It is grey and grimy outside, crowded and cluttered inside, and badly in need of several coats of paint, but the parents whose children go there have the highest praise for the place.

> We have children in from local schools to mix with ours and they carry them around, put them in chairs, brush their hair, put their coats on. If you ask them why they are doing this, they say, 'because he is handicapped'. I know they are acting out of kindness but it is infuriating when my staff are trying to make a child independent and will wait 20 minutes if necessary for him to put his coat on himself.
>
> And it isn't only the children. You get the same attitude from teachers in mainstream education. I was in a class recently which had a little Down's boy in it and the teacher told me, 'He's so affectionate. He puts his arms out for you to pick him up.'
>
> 'And what do you do?' I asked.
>
> 'I pick him up.'
>
> 'Do you pick up the other children?'
>
> 'No.'
>
> Of course not. The Down's boy also had a little nap in the afternoon. Did the other children? Certainly not. If he was at this school we would be struggling to make him as normal as possible. They were treating him as if he was completely different.

Paul Thomas also tells of a child who had been to an ordinary nursery before joining the school:

> He was the most withdrawn child I've ever met. There was no communication. He just sat in a corner. He's fine now, bright and friendly, but he'd be even further on if we'd had him from the start. The risk of putting children with severe learning difficulties into mainstream education is that they either become withdrawn or they are smothered into helplessness.
>
> I don't mean that our children shouldn't mix with others. We have integration programmes with 2 local schools whereby the children share some activities. Art and music, for instance, work very well. It's very stimulating in small doses, but we need our special schools.

Parents' views are as divided as teachers'. Some, particularly parents of very young children, see special schools as an unacceptable label and hope their children will attend 'normal' school. Others fear the bullying or teasing that they feel might be directed at a child who was different, and want a more protected environment.

John and Linda, whose 9-year-old son is integrated into a mainstream class, demonstate the opposing views. He feels that his son is getting the best possible chance to achieve his educational potential, and is, incidentally, educating the non-handicapped children to understand and accept the less able.

Linda, on the other hand, feels sad that her son is no longer 'special'. He has stopped getting the little treats that were available at his special school, such as being taken horse riding. She says she has no idea what he does at school all day and misses the involvement and easy familiarity with staff and other parents that she enjoyed at her son's old school.

As always, the ideal is choice; giving parents the chance to choose special schools, to opt for mainstream or to compromise with a special unit close to the ordinary school and the opportunity for plenty of social integration. Some enlightened education authorities are working towards this ideal but for most people it will still be a case of fighting for what you want or accepting what is available in your areas.

TALKING IT OUT – PARENTS' GROUPS

Parents' groups seem to be particularly appreciated at this stage, though for 'parents' read 'mothers'. Men rarely turn up to parents' group meetings. Often they can't because the meetings tend to be held in the daytime when they are at work. I only heard of one fathers' group, made up of men whose children attended a short-stay unit, and it had disbanded by the time I caught up with it.

'In any case,' the organizer's wife told me, 'it was never a group like we'd know it, not like mothers getting together and discussing their children or their feelings. This was just a few men who met in the pub and talked about football or whatever. I don't think they ever spoke about their children. They'd have thought that was weak or self-indulgent.'

A headteacher who sometimes recruits a voluntary labour force of fathers to help with running repairs to the school, found that the men did talk about their children, among other things, when they got together. 'It tended to be on the level of "Mine's a little a so-and-so, what's yours like?" It's a start.'

Women in groups however, talk, listen, empathize and sometimes become close friends. One of the problems is that, though they don't intend it, a group can become so close and cliquey that other mothers won't join it. 'I don't think I'd ever have had such good friends if it hadn't been for my daughter being handicapped,' a mother in one of the groups remarked.

Another mother of a teenage daughter insisted that having other women to talk to had saved her sanity. She needed to pour out her feelings and frustrations and her husband simply didn't want to discuss their daughter or the emotional and practical problems relating to her. It was not a unique situation. Other women admitted that they didn't actually know what their husbands thought about having a handicapped child. The men, mostly caring husbands and fathers, couldn't see any point in deep discussions. So the women brought their worries to the group for sharing.

A lot of information about benefits and the caring agencies was passed on in this way too. Several families said that most of the information they had came from other parents. I came across groups held in schools, in local MENCAP headquarters, under the auspices of the charity Contact-a-Family, and one longstanding group meeting in each other's homes, followed up by lunch in a restaurant.

They first met as a group of lonely young mothers in a small town who regularly bumped into each other at clinics and welfare centres with their children, and had become firm friends.

The groups vary in what they offer: anything from coffee and a chat, to guest speakers, or visits to somewhere of specialized interest, like a residential unit. Usually one or two parents do the organizing themselves, but Paul Thomas usually sits in on the meetings at his school, held in a classroom when the class is out:

> I do it to get the discussion going, to encourage people to open up. It's been very enlightening. One of the saddest things to come out of it is how little help and support the women feel they get from their partners. Another revelation is the way the mothers see themselves as unimportant. They view their husband as the breadwinner and therefore important, but see themselves as just skivvies. I try to show them that they possess many skills and to realize that it is they, not the professionals, who know their child best, and who help them most. I really do believe educating a child with learning difficulties is a partnership between school and parents. Meeting the mothers in this way has helped me to get to know them very well. I just wish more parents would come along to meetings.

Sue, who helps to organize this group's meetings, wishes they would too. She'd particularly like to see more Asian and black parents like herself: 'Although they appreciate everything the school is doing, they see it as somewhere quite separate their child goes and nothing to do with them. It's probably a cultural thing.'

Another reason may be that some of the mothers, whatever their ethnic origins, work and are not free to attend. Sue herself works as a nurse, with the combined help of a local respite unit, a relative and a self-employed husband who tries to fit his working hours around hers. It plainly takes some organizing, and, Sue says, she encounters disapproval from people who feel that she should devote all her time to looking after her 7-year-old hyperactive son. 'But I worked before my two sons were born, I enjoy it, so why should I stop now?' she says. She always tries to keep the morning of the parents' meeting free though.

> I can remember the first day Matt went to school as if it was yesterday. I was in a state of shock. I knew he had a mental handicap

but I don't think it hit me till I sat him going off to a special school
on special transport. I saw down and wept. The future looked awful.
I desperately needed to talk to someone who had a child like Matt
and understood, but I knew nobody. I really believed I was the only
person in the world with a child like mine and feelings like mine.

Of course when I joined the group and met the other mums, I
realized there were a lot of us in the same boat. And it does help just
to know that. There are people there I can talk freely in front of, cry
in front of if need be. We laugh a lot and enjoy a joke, but there's
always a shoulder to cry on.

PATTERNS

Is there a common pattern in the way parents feel at certain ages
and stages of their children's lives? I think so. The parents of
younger schoolchildren were more optimistic, more hopeful, more
open to accepting the positive attitude encouraged by the school.
Their children, they believed, were improving and would continue
to improve.

As children grow older, parents seem to become more resigned to
their limitations. They talk more of hoping the situation won't
deteriorate, than of expected improvements. In some there was a
disappointment that education hadn't delivered all it had promised

Parents of teenagers were anxious about where they would go
when schooldays ended. However they felt about a school, leaving
it was a frightening step into the unknown. Would there be a place
at the local day centre? The shortage of places in most areas is well
known. Would their child be helped there? Would she or he fit in
and enjoy it?

Some parents whose children had attended the same school right
up until the age of 19, were certain it was time for a change. 'It's not
that the school is bad, but he's bored to death with the same old
routine every day,' one mother explained. 'He hates going now. All
children should change school at around 11 years old.'

Carole, a young widow, explained how she gets her reluctant
16-year-old on to the school bus each day.

When I call him in the morning, the first thing he says, sort of
hopefully, is 'no school?' I say 'no school' because otherwise he won't

get up. I dress him. He can do it himself, but he takes so long he'd miss the bus. He thinks he's getting ready for a day dossing in front of the telly. I lie to him right up to the moment I get him outside on the doorstep. I feel a bit bad about it, but now I'm on my own, there's no other way to get him to do something he doesn't like. He's too big to force.

Many of the older mothers were facing the same mid-life traumas as most of their contemporaries, but having a child with a mental handicap intensified it. Maureen, for instance, dreads being left with only her handicapped son at home when the youngest of her two other boys leave. It's not the practical help she will miss, but the company, the noise, the liveliness. The nest will be almost empty but she still won't have the opportunity to stretch her wings. Other women talked of growing resentment at the prospect of lifelong mothering. 'Losing all the fun parts of being a mum and being left with the hard parts,' as one put it.

A social worker (interviewed on p.169), who grew up with a sister with a mental handicap, spoke of the way the 'normal evolution' of family life ceased for his parents. The able children left, leaving them isolated and lonely, but they could not revert to being a couple because of his sister.

There were a few who believed their own mother's diagnosis over the medical profession's, but on the whole the parents of the younger schoolchildren were the most informed about their child's condition of any I spoke to. Perhaps this is another tribute to their close links with their children's teachers and other professionals encountered at the school.

Not that they were over-impressed by these professionals. They welcomed a name and a number to contact in an emergency, but most only wanted people like social workers to come into their lives by invitation and had a dread of being 'taken over' by them. They still tended to see the school as the first place to go with a problem.

The help most valued by the parents, particularly of older schoolchildren, was respite care, whether it was provided in a local home, by another family in a system known as short-term fostering, shared care or under a variety of other titles, or by a care assistant who came into their own home and took over the care.

Not everyone had access to each system of respite care, however. Some didn't like what was available in their area; others felt they could, or should, cope without sending their child away. Some parents of teenagers were anxious about what would be available when they crossed that arbitrary boundary into adulthood. Children are better catered for with respite care, despite the fact that as parents get older they need more breaks. Likewise able people have more facilities available to them than those with multiple handicaps or challenging behaviour. It's the old 'Catch 22' of welfare services; the greater the need the less help is available.

In several cases, mothers had difficulty persuading fathers to let the child go away from home even for a weekend. Jane, the diminutive mother of a multi-handicapped only child in his teens, Jonathan, had never been able to convince her doctor husband:

> My husband is devoted to Jonathan and he's found the idea impossible to accept. If he could be convinced that it was for Jon's good he'd probably agree, but to do it just to give ourselves a break is not on. It's a pity but it's too late now. Perhaps if I'd started as I meant to go on when Jon was a small child . . .

Having a handicapped child undoubtedly puts an additional strain on a marriage, but a surpising number of parents claimed that the shared sorrow had brought them together, rather than pushing them apart. There was a commonly held belief that it does either one or the other, but the evidence is that, for the majority of people, it does neither and they just struggle along facing the ups and downs like any couple.

The biggest complaint about husbands was that they refused to discuss their feelings about the handicapped child and left all the decisions to their wives. Another grumble was that it took fathers far longer to accept there was anything wrong with the child. Out at work all day, they saw less of the child and believed their wife was neurotically inventing problems. 'Or at least I preferred to believe she was inventing it,' one man admitted.

Some couples who might otherwise separate, stay together for the sake of the child. They may adapt to the situation by leading separate lives, one going out while the other baby sits. ('But guess who goes out most often?' said one mother, cynically). A headteacher who sees this happen again and again encourages parents to go out together at least once a week, putting them in touch with an agency that can provide a trained sitter, 'Otherwise they drift apart and that's not much of a marriage.'

SPEAKING FOR THEMSELVES

JOANNA

Cathy and Chris have reels of home movies of Joanna as a baby. Joanna sitting on the beach, aged 9 months, fascinated by the pebbles around her. . . . Joanna, bright and pretty, splashing in the sea . . . Joanna beaming at family and friends from her mother's lap, a happy, healthy baby.

The filming stops abruptly when she is a year old. 'We lost enthusiasm for recording her progress,' her father, Chris, says, wryly. When they resumed again, a few years later, Joanna was a very different child. Gone is the look of bright-eyed interest. Joanna totters a few steps, stiff-legged, arms raised, then falls down. She makes strange jerky movements. She constantly wrings her hands. She is almost unrecognizable from the bonny baby who promised so much.

Joanna (aged 6) suffers from Rett's Syndrome, an incurable brain disorder, which affects girls only and results in profound mental and physical handicaps. The cruellest trick the condition plays is that it allows children to develop normally for around the first year of life, then snatches away the skills they have learned.

Rett's Syndrome was only identified in the early 1980s. Not only had Cathy and Chris never heard of it, neither, it seems, had the professionals they met. Joanna's regression bewildered everyone. Chris works in insurance and the family live in a new house in an affluent suburb.

Cathy: 'The change started at about 9 months. She'd been saying words, playing like my friends' babies and she just stopped. I told them at the clinic, but they said babies go through phases where they learn a lot and phases where they seem to stop for a while. What I couldn't get through to people was that this was not a pause in development, but regression.

'Then, at 15 months, she had measles and she came out of that completely different. She was so withdrawn that if you put her favourite toys beside her, she didn't even notice them. All she did was lie on the floor and rub her lip, just this one repetitive movement. I kept telling people but nobody would take any notice. She's a pretty child and when I'd take her to the doctor, she'd sit up and respond well because she loves people, and I think he and others were blinded by this.

'One day she had what looked like a fit – her eyes rolled up in her head. The doctor came and said, "Children do that sometimes." I was absolutely terrified. I was searching library shelves for a book that might say something about her symptoms. I found one that said dribbling and teeth grinding were signs of mental handicap. Joanna did both, but I couldn't accept that. I thought if you had a child with a mental handicap they knew at birth. I was obsessed with making her walk, as if this would somehow prove she was alright. I'd spend all day getting her up on her feet, and eventually she did totter, after a fashion, but she was still way behind other babies in every other way.'

Chris: 'We were having arguments. Cathy was at home with Joanna all day so she could see what she was like. Being out at work, I saw less. I wanted to believe Cathy was over reacting.'

Cathy: 'I got to the stage where I didn't dare mention her peculiar bits of behaviour to Chris because it annoyed him. I began to believe I was imagining it, so when she started to raise her eyebrows, I said nothing Then Chris said to me, "I wonder why she keeps raising her eyebrows?"'

Chris: 'The first person really to notice she was behind was the play therapist who came round after Cathy had pestered everyone. She arrived with toys suitable for an 18-month old, which Joanna couldn't cope with at all. She went out to her car and came back with baby toys. All she said was, "Better go back to basics", but it was chilling.'

The family was referred to a child development centre, and from there they got an appointment with a paediatrician.

Cathy: 'We sat down and he spoke to us for about three minutes. Then he said, "Well, you've got a significantly handicapped child here." I just wanted to die. I wanted to throw myself out of the window. What I'd hoped he'd say was "Your child's got this problem, but we can do this or that and put it right." I wanted them to make her better and he was telling me they couldn't.'

Chris: 'It was shattering, yes, and an abrupt way of finding out, but to me it was almost a relief. It took us off the see-saw of hope and doubt. We knew there was a genuine problem.'

Cathy: 'They took her into hospital for tests, to try and find out exactly what was wrong with her. I remember looking at these other parents, fussing over their children, and thinking, "I wish mine only had a broken leg or diabetes."'

It was eventually Cathy and Chris themselves who diagnosed their daughter's condition, and told the doctors.

Cathy: 'We were watching television and there was a 30-second public service broadcast for a charity called the Rett's Syndrome Association. They started describing children who were just like Joanna, even down to the wringing of the hands and rubbing the lip. We sent off for their literature and when it came back, well, it could have been written about Joanna.'

Chris: 'It wasn't a pleasant read. It told us about the problems we would have in the future, like joints becoming deformed and curvature of the spine. It put paid to any lingering hope that she was going to get better, but at least we knew we weren't alone. We went to a conference on the syndrome and bumped into our paediatrician. I told him I thought Joanna had got Rett's and after the conference he came over and said he agreed with our diagnosis.

'Having a label took away the guilt. We used to go through everything that had ever happened, searching for a reason. Was it the forceps delivery? Was it the time she fell down the stairs? Once you realize it's genetic, it's predestined in a way.'

3-year-old Sara was born before Joanna's condition was diagnosed, and although they have been told that the chance of another affected child is low, they won't be adding to their family.

Cathy: 'You become aware of the hundreds of things that could go wrong, even if not this particular one. It frightens you. Having Joanna has changed me in many ways. I'm much more confident because I've had to fight to get people to listen to me and to get Joanna her rights. And I do feel a bit bitter. You know — why us?'

Chris: 'We've not asked for much from the welfare services, so I was very annoyed when they made a fuss over letting us have a particular pushchair. They tried to palm us off with a really ugly wheelchair — it might as well have a label on it saying 'severely handicapped child'. In the end we got the one we wanted. It costs £830 but it is very comfortable and sturdy, just right for her. And they can have it back to use for another child when she's finished with it.

'We've coped better than I thought we would. Once we knew where we stood, we pulled together. The problem is that if you are coping everyone assumes you'll go on doing so and you don't get offers of help.'

Cathy: 'Our families dote on her. Everyone thinks she smiles and claps only for them, but in fact she does it for everyone. We can usually get someone from the family to babysit, but there's nobody we could leave her with for, say, a week. My sister's offered but she couldn't cope. People don't really understand what's involved in looking after her. It looks easier from the outside.'

Joanna has had several overnight stays and one weekend in a short stay home run by a voluntary agency.

Cathy: 'It's very hard to bring yourself to take her in and leave her. She may not be unhappy there, but you know she'll be less happy than at home. When she was away for the weekend, we made a point of going away with Sara. It was unbelievable how easy it was doing things without a handicapped child. There wasn't this permanent anxiety; you could do things on the spur of the moment and you didn't have to drag all the paraphenalia and equipment around. Sara loves her sister but she had such a good time she didn't want to come home. She's had to grow up quickly. We expect a lot of her for her age.'

A holiday in France with Joanna, last year, was a disaster.

Cathy: 'She has to have her routine or she gets upset and screams and cries all the time. We drove 750 miles in one day to get home quickly. But we couldn't get her into the short-stay home this summer so we're taking her to Majorca. She's changed a bit; she's calmer this year. We hope it will be okay. Maybe next year we'll get something arranged in time. We're interested in applying for the short-term fostering scheme, where she would be looked after by a family. I prefer the sound of that, though I don't think I'll ever get over worrying about her when she's away.

'The one place I know she loves is school. It's a scruffy little school for children with severe learning difficulties, in a fairly rough area. We could have got her into a beautiful new school nearer home but I didn't take to the headmistress. I trust the headteacher and the staff at Joanna's school 160 per cent. The only time I'm not thinking about her is when she's there. If there was a respite unit attached to the school, I'd be happy to let her stay there.'

MARK

Mark is 9 years old and the eldest of four children. He has Down's Syndrome. His parents, John and Linda, were only 19 when he was born. They have lived for 8 months on a new estate tacked onto a village. John works as a maintenance engineer in the nearest town.

Linda: 'At first we decided we weren't going to keep him. The doctor who told us he has Down's made us an appointment with a social worker, and she told us that if we didn't want him we could have him fostered, and then adopted when a suitable family came along. We thought about it and said yes, that's what we wanted.'

John: 'Linda wanted to keep him really but I wasn't sure, and our families kept going on about how young we were and how we'd never be able to look after a handicapped kid. Everyone said it would ruin our lives. It seemed the sensible thing at the time, having him fostered. We knew nothing about handicapped children. We didn't even know what Down's Syndrome was.'

Linda: 'Mark was born on a Sunday and they told us on the Thursday morning. They made an appointment for us to see the paediatrician. Mark was brought up from the Special Care Unit and we took him into the doctor's office with us.

'The doctor started talking about Down's Syndrome and chromosomes and we just sat there, looking at him. We didn't know what he was telling us. He must have twigged because he mentioned mongolism and then we knew. All I remember after that was John in tears and me asking whether my son would ever get married. What a stupid question.'

John: 'You don't know what to say. You're going along fine, quite happy, and then the floor just disappears from under you.'

Linda: 'Mark looked so normal, just like any baby. I kept expecting someone to come up and say "Sorry, there's been a mistake, he's normal after all." Friends kept saying he looked okay to them and sort of agreeing that the doctors might have been wrong. I'm sure people do this out of kindness but it just raises false hopes. It would have been better if they'd been brutally honest.'

The doubts evaporated when the social worker brought up the subject of adoption.

Linda: 'I wasn't really surprised by the suggestion. It just seemed like another option. During the two weeks he was in the special care unit John and I tried hard not to get involved with him. John didn't even visit. But it was still heartbreaking for me when they took him off to the foster mother's.

'I started visiting him there. I just couldn't break off contact, but nobody would come with me. My mother did at first, but then she stopped because she said it was too painful when we weren't going to keep him. I needed to see him though, to be sure he was all right.

'Then the foster family decided to go on holiday for two weeks and the social worker asked if we'd look after Mark while they were away. There was no pressure; she said they could place him in short-term care if we weren't agreeable, but John is convinced it was deliberate ploy to push us together with the baby and create a bond.'

John: 'And it worked, didn't it? Linda talked me into having Mark for the two weeks. She was so excited I couldn't refuse. The amazing thing was how our families – the very people who told us keeping him would ruin our lives – reacted once he was here, a real flesh and blood baby.

'We told everyone it was only for two weeks, but they still insisted on buying him presents and saying how lovely he was. I suppose a baby is a baby. I knew Linda wanted to keep him and by the end of the foster family's holiday, so did I. Having him around all the time, I just got attached. He never went back.'

Did they, I wondered, ever regret that decision?

Linda: 'Momentarily, but the feeling doesn't last. He's part of the family now. Life would have been easier without him. We didn't realize what we were letting ourselves in for. He wasn't far behind other children when he was a baby, but the gap gets wider and wider. It's sad to watch our other children overtaking him. Even the baby, at two, can do most of the things Mark can.

'He's got a lovely personality. Everyone thinks he's lovely and cuddly but they don't see the other side of him. He'll sit in front of the telly all day and eat without stopping and it's so frustrating when he doesn't understand simple instructions. Our friends love him, but they also say if they had one like him they wouldn't keep him.

'The neighbours around here accept him completely, but strangers, people in the street, they stare as if he's some kind of oddity. Sometimes I can ignore it, others I'm in tears. My mum and my sister are terrible. They are really rude to anyone they catch glancing in Mark's direction. I just feel protective. I want to get him out of the way.'

John: 'People looking at him don't bother me. Before we had Mark, I used to stare myself if I saw anyone out of the ordinary. It's natural, isn't it?'

Mark now attends a mainstream school, which fully integrates children with severe learning difficulties into normal classes.

Linda: 'We were amazed when we moved here and heard that this was the policy, that he'd be attending a normal school right through till he leaves. They have up to two children with special needs per class and an extra teacher just for them. They stay with their age group and do the same subjects, though simpler things.

'John thinks it's great. He says with a teacher to himself, Mark is getting the chance to develop at the maximum rate. And he's getting used to normal children while they are getting to know children with handicaps. I don't know, though – it seems to me that Mark is no longer treated as special. He's lost some of the opportunities he had at special school – like going horse-riding with people who understood him.

'At his special school, the parents were involved. You got to know the teachers and exactly what they are doing with your child, and you were welcome to go in at any time. Now I just put him on the bus in the morning and get him off again in the evening. I've no idea what he does at school. There was a parents' night, which I couldn't get to, but in any case I wouldn't have felt comfortable there with all the parents of normal kids.

'John and I have always had a different attitude to Mark and to handicap. He prefers to stay away from the whole business, but I like to be involved. It used to cause arguments, but now we just agree to differ. I was involved in everything at the special school, though the first time I visited it I nearly died of shock.

'They took me round the special care unit and there was a big lad of 19 there, with a beard, just lying on the floor in a nappy. And you think, "Will my child end up like that?" It didn't take me long to get to know the kids and their parents though, and to realize the ones I'd thought of as vegetables were real people with personalities of their own.'

John: 'Linda tells people about Mark. I don't mention it unless I have to. If someone asks me I say I've got four kids, not three and one handicapped. I just realized the other day that the manager in the company where I've worked for 7 years didn't know about Mark. There was no reason why he should.'

John and Linda were pleased with the help they had from a visiting teacher before Mark started school, and they are happy to see their local community nurse once a month.

Linda: 'We didn't want a social worker, because they are nosey and delve into everything in your life, not just the child's problems. Information about allowances and that, I mostly learned from other mothers at Mark's first school. That's where I heard about the Family Fund. It's been a lot of help. We've had a washing machine and a tumble dryer and they've paid for a couple of holidays for the whole family. I suppose we apply for something every two years. We've never been turned down. What makes me mad though is the attitude from some of our family that we're lucky getting these perks, that we do very well out of it. Don't they realize we'd give back everything if we could make Mark a normal child?'

EMMA

Emma, now aged 7, has severe multiple handicaps. She is the oldest of three children. Her brother, Peter, is 6, her baby sister, Maria, 10 months. Trish, her mother, was 18 when Emma was born; her father, Owen, a warehouseman, was 21. Trish says she knew very little about babies, even less about the problems that could beset them.

Trish: 'It was a long labour, a terrible birth. I only realized how bad when I came to have my second baby. I thought everyone went through what I suffered with Emma. I should have had a Caesarean. My mum has always claimed Emma would have been alright if they'd done one straight away and not let me go on and on.

'Emma wasn't breathing at first. I didn't get to see her. They whisked her away and put me to sleep for 6 hours. They said she had tummy ache. They kept a lot from us. She'd actually started fitting.

'She was in special care for 10 days and they did an EEC and a brain scan. They didn't seem to know what was wrong with her. At one point they asked me if I'd been taking drugs or sniffing glue. I was gobsmacked. I'd never even taken a pill from the doctor. After 10 days we were allowed to take her home with just some drugs for the fits.

'I had no idea there were going to be any serious long-term problems. Nobody said. But in the back of my mind I think I knew it wasn't just something she was going to get over. I just didn't like to think about it.

'During the next couple of months we took her back to the hospital for checkups – Owen always had time off work and came with me. At this one appointment when she was 12 weeks, the doctor called us into his office. There was another doctor with him and about a dozen other people, probably students, and before we could sit down, he told us that the scan had shown Emma had brain damage. What I remember most is the way he blurted it out without even asking us to sit down and these twelve paris of eyes staring, waiting for some sort of reaction.

'I don't know if they got the reaction they expected. I didn't feel anything except shock. When we got outside I was starting to feel angry and resentful towards Emma herself, as if she'd let me down. Owen said, "Don't you start writing her off just because that lot in there have." He went back to work and I went round to my mum's. Mum started crying and that set me off. I don't think it sunk in till then.

'The doctors didn't really know what had caused the damage. At first they thought it was genetic, then they said it was just a freak of nature, then they decided it was caused by a virus. We still think she could have been damaged by the birth, or by the fact that she was so overdue.

'The next couple of years were dreadful. We dreaded taking Emma back to the hospital. Every time we did they had something else to tell us – she'd be in nappies all her life, she wouldn't feed herself, she wouldn't walk. I felt very bitter. I used to think "Why me? Why us? What have we done?" But it never came between Owen and me. It brought us closer. Once we started accepting it, once we started pulling together and getting on with life, it was easier.

'The doctors at the hospital suggested we should have another baby right away. We took their advice. It was hinted, though they didn't come right out and say it, that as we were so young, we should put Emma away and start again. But of course we never considered that and what happened was that, when Emma was 21 months old, I was at home trying to look after two completely dependent babies, her and Peter. It was like having twins, who were developing in completely different ways. Just feeding Emma took up half the day, and there was the constant worry of her getting ill.

'She was in and out of hospital all the time; eight times in her first year. They kept warning us she wasn't going to live. When I look back I wonder how I got through that time. I was so exhausted and depressed I thought I was going nutty and I couldn't tell anyone, except a community nurse who used to call and would try to help. Most people acted as if I should be able to cope; "Good old Trish, she can cope with anything." I felt I had to live up to people's ideas of me. But they didn't understand what Emma was like. She cried non-stop for 3 years. When Peter was very tiny I used to have to put her down in her cot upstairs and let her cry. Otherwise I'd just have gone mad. Owen would walk in from work and I'd hand the two of them to him. I felt as if I was in a deep hole and every time I tried to get out, something pushed me back in. I relied completely on him taking over.

'Then, when I was absolutely at rock bottom, Owen was taken into hospital with meningitis. I thought I'd collapse, but what happened was that it bucked me up. When he wasn't there, I had to stand alone. I'd had some anti-depressant pills from the doctor because I was desperate to get back to my normal self, but during the time Owen was ill, I flushed the lot down the toilet and never needed them again.

'One of the biggest worries has been Emma's health and it hasn't been made any better by the hospital always expecting her to die and warning us not to expect to take her home. She's always been a very poor feeder and sometimes, when she was younger, she just wouldn't suck. We've had to find ways of getting her bottle down her. At one stage we were feeding her with a syringe. Then we found that if we melted a bit of milky bar and smeared it on the top of the teat she'd let it in her mouth and take one suck. Once she's started she'll carry on with the rest of the bottle.

'Except for Attendance Allowance which I was told about at the hospital, I've found out about other help through talking to other mums like the ones I met at the monthly coffee morning at Emma's school. Even something as basic as the free disposable nappies you can get when a child is 2, I wasn't officially told about. I don't say we've had a worse deal than any other parents. Talking to other mothers you find out the welfare services aren't very good at communicating.

'We manage okay now, even with the latest addition, Maria, who's 10 months, because I've got a routine. When Emma gets home on the minibus at 3.30, she has a drink, then her tea, and she lies down or sits in her chair till about 6.30. She likes to have music on, but she can't do much. She has to be fed and she's incontinent and can't sit up unaided. At 6.30 I start getting her ready for bed, wash her, give her the tablet for her fits and another drink, and she goes up around 7.30. In fact what usually happens now is that Owen gets Emma ready for bed while I deal with the baby. Owen is great with her. He washes and dresses her at the weekend and when he's home, looks after her as much as I do. We get the children to bed so that we can have a few hours together. That's very important to us. You can end up having no time at all for each other, and that benefits nobody in the end.

'Friends and neighbours have always been very good. Sometimes a friend will say "Oh, I'll look after Emma for a few hours", but I know she couldn't. The mistake I made was refusing offers of help when she was little, on the grounds that I'd have to cope with her so I might as well learn. If people had got used to dealing with her when she was a baby, they'd be able to help now.

'We do get a break because Emma goes into respite care one weekend a month. She stays in a bungalow with just three other children and she loves it. We've had this weekend break now for 4 years. I had a lot of trouble talking Owen into it at first. He didn't want anyone else looking after her, taking his place, and he thought it wasn't right we should do it for our benefit. Once he saw Emma is happy and it's for her benefit too, he was fine.'

PAUL

Ten-year-old Paul has an extra tail on his 15th chromosome, a genetic condition so rare that at the time of diagnosis, he was thought to be the only child in Britain suffering from it. No other child with this abnormality has survived longer than 3 years, but since Paul is only 50 per cent affected, nobody knows his life expectancy.

He is the oldest of four children. His father, Carl, is an exhibition carpenter who works away from home a good deal, leaving his mother, Helen, to cope alone. They live in a 3-bedroomed city semi which they are trying to sell to buy a four-bedroomed house in the same area. Paul has always had to have a room of his own.

Helen: 'Paul can do quite a lot – he can feed himself, he can walk when he feels like it. He has no trouble letting you know what he wants and he's very affectionate.'

At this point, Paul, sitting beside his mother, leaned over to hug her, as if to demonstrate, while his two small brothers and sister played in the next room.

Helen: 'The problem is he's so mischievous. You never know what he's going to do next. Yesterday he took a dislike to my lovely sunflowers in the garden and broke them in half. He'll pull the leaves off the houseplants one by one. The other night there was a smell of burning in his room, and I traced it to the bowl-shaped shade on his light. He'd squeezed all his socks in there and they were smouldering.'

Perhaps Paul's worst piece of 'mischief' is his habit of smearing faeces on every available surface, and on himself, given the chance.

Helen: 'It'll be all over the window, in his hair, everywhere. There's no way you can persuade him not to do something. Smacking has no effect. The most successful method is to tell him he's a naughty boy and ignore him for half-an-hour. He hates that. It might deter him for a while, but not always.'

Despite all this, Helen plainly adores her eldest son.

Helen: 'If I could change him for a normal, undamaged Paul, I wouldn't. The only thing I'd change is that I'd like him to be able to talk. Just this week he's started using a few words of Makaton, the sign language they teach them at school. He's been signing "toilet" and "biscuit". It's quite emotional, like a normal child's first words.'

Though Paul was born 8 weeks prematurely, the first sign that he had a handicap came when he developed severe fits at 5 months old. He was rushed to hospital.

Helen: 'We were told by a doctor with a smile on his face as if he was giving the weather forecast, that if our son survived the operation they planned for him tomorrow, he would be a vegetable.

'Next morning they'd changed their mind about the operation. He hadn't got what they thought after all. A genetics expert was called in. It took some time to find out what was wrong. She didn't exactly say outright that he would die by the time he was three, but it was obvious that was what she expected.

'Like everything else we were told, it was wrong. We were told he'd be a cabbage, that he'd have fits all the time, that he'd have no muscle tone and never walk. The truth is nobody knows what will happen with Paul. He's a one-off. Every time he gets ill, I try to prepare myself for the end. We take him to see a specialist once a year and I want to ask how long he thinks Paul has, but I'm afraid to because I might not like the answer.'

Because her husband's work takes him away a lot, Helen, who's not yet thirty, often has to cope on her own.

Helen: 'It used to frighten me, being alone, and I used to resent it, but I've changed. I cope better on my own. I do things at my own pace. Carl reacts very badly to the mess ordinary children make. He's only seen the result of Paul's smearing once. I rush round like a mad thing cleaning up, so that he won't see.

'Paul doesn't want anything to do with his father. If Carl gives him a kiss, he'll say "yuck" and sit in the corner, silent and resentful. I don't know if this hurts Carl. I don't know what he feels about Paul, full stop. He hardly ever talks to me about him. Just once or twice when Paul is coming up to a birthday, he's said, "I wonder what he'd be like if he was normal". I've heard him telling other people, like the medical students who have been sent to see Paul because his condition is so rare, that I have a lot to cope with. But he's never told me.

The only time I've seen my husband lose control was the night they told us Paul might not get through the operation when he was a baby. He turned away and I could see he was crying, but when I went to him, he stopped immediately. He'll always comfort me though. His attitude is to let me have a good cry and get it out of my system. He's miserable if he's not up to his eyes with work. I think work is his way of coping.'

Helen and Carl were told that there was a risk of other children in the family being born with the same condition as Paul, but they decided to go ahead and add to their family anyway.

Helen: 'I had amniocentesis with the middle two, but I was 24 weeks pregnant before the results came through. I don't know if I could have gone through with a termination at that stage. Fortunately I never had to make the decision. I didn't even have the test with the last baby, Carrie, who's two.'

While Helen talked to me, Andrew, her 6-year-old, was in charge of his little brother and sister. She is aware of the amount of responsibility that falls on his frail shoulders.

Helen: 'He's had to grow up before his time. Sometimes I'll hear Carl say to him, "You look after the little ones", and I think, "He's only a little one himself."

'Andrew has had problems at school. The other children used to see Paul when I went up to collect him and they started laughing at him and taking the mickey. The teachers were very good. When they realized what was going on, they made up an assembly about a little boy who was special, and had Andrew talk about Paul.

'He stood up and said that Jesus hadn't made Paul properly – just as I'd told him. His teacher says that now she knows about Paul, she understands Andrew better. He needs a lot of affection. But I know he gets less of my attention than he deserves. I've started having someone come in to sit with the others after school one afternoon a week, while I take him swimming, just me and him.'

Paul has been awarded mobility allowance because of his fits and his limited walking ability, and Helen is determined to learn to drive so that she can take the four children out together.

She has the number of a social worker if she has any problems.

Helen: 'But the last time I contacted him was four or five years ago. I'd hate to have someone dropping in regularly, telling me how to do things. It's the same with a respite care home. I know the place is there if I have an emergency, but I won't let him go otherwise.

'I sent him there once for what was supposed to be a weekend. But after a day I fetched him home. There's nothing wrong with the place and Paul was quite happy. It was me. I missed him so much. The house just doesn't feel right without him.'

ADAM

Adam, a blond, angelic-looking 7-year old, has had a variety of labels pinned on him in his short life – autistic, mentally handicapped, dyslexic, aphasic. His parents, Gerry and Kay, accept only the last one. They believe their son suffers from aphasia, or speech impairment, and that he may have a 'mental impairment' not a mental handicap.

He was born with a club foot 'and problems down the left side of his body as if he'd had a stroke'. His slowness in speech and behavioural problems began when he was 2 years old. At the moment, Adam attends a mainstream school with extra classroom help. He has an 11-year-old sister, Lisa.

Gerry: 'The top and tail of the matter is that nobody really knows what is wrong with Adam. One psychologist admitted he'd never seen another child like him, which is pretty scary.

'He can speak but never holds conversations. He just uses clichés and odd phrases. Once, he had a very painful operation on his foot and he wouldn't let the doctors near him afterwards; he was fighting and screaming, "You'll never take me alive." It made sense in the circumstances, but I wonder what the medical staff thought. And yet he knows so much. I remember showing him a picture book when he was little and pointing out a spaceman. He said, "You mean an astronaut." I didn't think he even knew the word.

'Most children with speech problems are desperate to communicate, but Adam doesn't seem to need friends. A lot of the time he lives in a world of his own. He is doing well at school work, but he doesn't mix with the other kids."

Kay: 'I was a bit apprehensive about him going to an ordinary school, but I didn't want him at a school for children with learning difficulties. We have to keep our options open though. When he's 10 or 11, the gap between him and the other children may be too wide.

'The thing that upsets me about the school is that he gets bullied. I've seen this on a coach when I've been on an outing with the class (they always need an extra pair of hands to cope with Adam) and in the playground when I go to pick him up. One boy in the playground had him in a corner and all Adam could think to do was try to put his arms around him. They tease him about talking and laughing to himself about the jargon he uses. He's different so he's bound to be singled out.

'We didn't know until recently whether or not he's aware of his handicaps. But recently a children's programme on television did an item on children with disabilities. They talked about how people sometimes couldn't speak properly and said you shouldn't laugh at them because it wasn't funny. Adam was glued to the screen. He turned round, very serious and said, "No, it isn't a bit funny, is it Mummy?"'

Gerry: 'On the other hand he looks so normal it's hard for people to understand there's a problem. Two years ago he had to have some blood taken for tests in hospital. As we walked in, I took off my jacket, ready to hold him down. The staff laughed. They thought they could just a have a few firm words with Adam and he would keep still. Of course he didn't. He screamed and fought, and in the end it took five of us to hold him down. After they'd finished I just sat by the bed and cried I was so drained.'

Kay: 'Fortunately Gerry and I can always talk things over, so having Adam hasn't pushed us apart. It has restricted our lives though, and Lisa's. She's been a second mother to him but now, coming up to adolescence she's losing patience. She doesn't understand why he won't behave normally. He embarrasses her in front of her friends.

'I feel guilty about the way Adam is. It goes round and round in my head – why did it happen? I took some medicine prescribed by the doctor when I was pregnant – could that have harmed him? As a baby, he used to cry for ages and sometimes I'd just have to put him down in his cot, still crying. One morning I went in and he was deathly white. I picked him up and he was okay, but could he have stopped breathing for a minute?

'I'm not quite as bad as I was, I used to drive Gerry mad. Do you think it was this? Could it have been that? I'm always amazed that parents like us don't get offerred counselling routinely. You have so many confused feelings to work through. You need to try and get your priorities straight. People won't let you talk about it. When Adam was little I used to take him to a mother-and-toddler group. When he behaved peculiarly, the other mothers would look at him and I'd say, "He has a handicap." They'd look shocked and say, "Oh, no, I'm sure he hasn't", and turn away.'

Gerry: 'Sometimes I look at Adam and feel really upset about the normal "little boy" things he'll miss — riding his bike, playing soldier games, fooling around with his friends. But then I remind myself that he doesn't miss these experiences. What I want most for him is that he's employable when he's grown up and can lead something like a normal life.'

Kay: 'I'd hate to give the impression that it's all doom and gloom. Adam has enriched our lives too. I'm not really religious, but I do feel that we may, somehow, have been chosen for him. We can cope, whereas some people might not. It feels absolutely right that we've got him.'

DARREN

Linda (36) lives in a small industrial town with her husband, Jim, and Darren aged 8. Jim, an ex lorry driver, is off work with a slipped disc, and hoping to retrain for a lighter job when he's recovered. Darren is their only child.

Linda: 'And that's the way it's going to stay. We'd have liked more children, but after Darren I'm too scared. They say it's nothing genetic but whatever went wrong the first time could go wrong again, couldn't it?'

I met her at her son's school. A group of children walked through the hall, Darren rushing ahead of them, a serious-looking little boy in grey flannels and spectacles.

Linda: 'Looks as if butter wouldn't melt in his mouth, doesn't he? But you should see him when he's having a temper tantrum. He's violent towards himself and to anybody who happens to be near. He'll scratch his chest till he fetches blood and if anyone is by him he'll scratch them too. The tantrums have always been his biggest problem. I don't know what causes them, nobody seems to know. I think it's anxiety and frustration. I know when one's coming. I can see the tension building up. When he was little he used to bang his head against a brick wall.

'The other awful problems are his obsessions. At the moment he's going through a spitting phase. At home he spits all the time. He even does it in his sleep so it's not something that's under his control. Before that it was switching lights on and off. On and off they went all day long. You couldn't stop him. You could tear your hair out. You have to tell yourself the phase will pass — but you know there will be another one, maybe even worse, to take its place.

'He's been much better since he's been at this school though (a school for children with severe learning difficulties). It broke my heart to let him come here. Before, he was at a school for children with moderate learning difficulties, but they didn't know how to deal with his behaviour. Every day they had some complaint. They never said anything good about him, and he hated going. He was always wanting to stay at home. It's not like that here. He's always been happy to come. At first I was frightened to come in or phone up. I'd be thinking "What's he done today?" But they've been marvellous; always positive, seeing his good points. There's a stigma attached to letting him come here. You're admitting he is very handicapped. But now I feel I was forcing him to go to a place he couldn't cope with for my own pride.

'Darren got off to a bad start. He was blue when he was born and had to be injected to start him breathing. He was in a cot beside my bed and, for the first two or three hours, he was whimpering as if he was in pain. They wouldn't let me feed him, so I asked the sister if she could give him something to drink. She started to give him a drop of glucose then she threw down the bottle and rushed off with him to find oxygen. He'd turned blue again.

'They told me he had breathing problems and when my husband came in they said he had low blood sugar, which was causing convulsions. They also said they didn't expect him to live. We had him baptised that night.

'But he pulled through, and they put this drain in his brain so that the drugs could get there direct, and after 3 or 4 days he stopped convulsing. Then the nursing officer took us into a room and told us that he'd probably be a cabbage because of the fits. That's exactly the word she used, cabbage. You don't forget something like that.

'I was too distressed to think much about the words she was using at the time. I remember saying no matter how bad he was we wanted him to live. They offered us a photograph they'd taken of him, but I didn't want a photograph; I wanted my son. They were very pessimistic. They said "He may not be able to suck, he may not take food." That was a laugh. When they allowed me to put him to the breast he started to suck as if he was ravenous, which he probably was. I went home that night at 7 p.m. and rang at 10 p.m. to see if he was okay, and a nurse said, "He drinks like a drain your son!" He came home at 11 days and it was like a miraculous recovery. A nurse who'd seen him just after birth and then saw him a month later couldn't believe it was the same baby.

'After being told how severely handicapped he was going to be, we were so involved in looking for the really bad signs, which didn't come, that we missed the small signs that he wasn't developing normally. Not having anything much to do with kids, he seemed normal to us and we began to think that a big, bad mistake had been made by the hospital and he was okay after all. But as he got older I started to compare him with other children. His mannerisms were different and I'd certainly never seen another child throw tantrums like Darren's. It was an emotional see-saw – we thought we had a normal baby at birth, then we were told he was a cabbage, then he seemed to be developing normally, then we realized he wasn't.

'My husband found it very hard to accept. He hates to think that Darren will never do the things he did as a lad, and he used to get very embarrassed when people stared. You'll be sitting on a bus and Darren will suddenly start waving his hands around or slapping his face or shouting out. I'm not bothered by other people's reactions any more. If they stare, I'll stare right back. He's not the only kid in the world who's different. Old people are the worst. They look at him as if he should be locked away. I suppose kids like him were in their day.

'He could have been worse. They thought he was blind at 8 months but, though he doesn't have perfect vision, he certainly can see. He's been wearing glasses since he was 23 months old – he used to cry when you put them on at first, but now if you forget he reminds you. The first time he had them on, he looked up and saw a bird. He was so excited.

'I've been given the name of a woman who deals with respite care, but I'm not sure we need it at the moment. We've always felt that, as Darren is the only one, we have time to look after him ourselves. My mum is a great help and I have an aunt I could call on if I needed someone to sit with him for a few hours. I can't take him shopping, for instance — he'd run away or pick up the fruit and eat it. Friends who've got kids sometimes offer to have him for a few days, but they don't really know what they'd be taking on. Would they be prepared to lie down on the bed with him for half an hour every night till he falls asleep? Otherwise he won't sleep.

'And he runs away. He managed to get out on to the busy street where we live just recently. We were running around looking for him, our hearts in our mouths, when he casually walked in. My mother says why don't we keep all the doors in house locked, but that's not teaching him. He has to understand what he can and can't do.

'Every day with Darren is stressful. There's no let-up 365 days a year. But I still feel the same as I did when they told me he was going to be badly handicapped 8 years ago — that he's mine and I want him with me, whatever.'

The following four children are older, though still at school. All four attend different schools, though Charlotte and Brian come from the same area.

KAREN

Seventeen-year-old Karen has severe multiple handicaps. She is totally dependent, has to be fed and is doubly incontinent. Her walking is also very poor, though her mother says she is not strictly physically handicapped. Karen lives at home with her parents Sue and Peter, and an older brother and younger sister.

Sue: 'From the time she was 16 months old, Karen's development just stood still. In some ways she regressed. As long as she was doing baby things she was okay, but she never got beyond that stage.

'It never occurred to me she might be mentally handicapped. I literally never gave it a thought. What did worry me was that she wasn't walking. She could crawl and sit up and she would walk round her playpen holding the bars, but the minute you took her out and tried to stand her up on the floor she shook all over. She seemed frightened and insecure.

'I took her to the doctor when she was 16 months and still not walking, but he said I was worrying too much. I accepted that, but a couple of weeks after, a friend with a little boy Karen's age came to see me and I was dumbstruck at the difference between the two children. He seemed so independent; Karen was just a baby by comparison. He was saying words meaningfully. Although Karen said "Mama" she never seemed to associate it with me.

'I still wasn't thinking in terms of mental handicap, but I went back to the doctor and said "Look, something is seriously wrong." This time he referred me to a clinic which I thought was a hearing and speech centre. He said she might have hearing problems but there was no mention of mental problems. He didn't warn me that the place was for children with all sorts of handicaps.

'At the centre, I was taken to see a psychologist who did some test with Karen, then said: "Mrs M . . . . . ., it's quite obvious that your daughter is mentally retarded."

'I was absolutely stunned. My first reaction was that this woman was mad. Karen looked perfectly normal and in the couple of months prior to this appointment she'd improved a lot. She'd even started walking, at 23 months, and I'd been so relieved.

'I had to pick my husband up from work, so I put Karen into the car, very calmly, and started to drive across town. Halfway there the psychologist's words sank in and I burst into tears. I don't know how I drove the car safely through the rush-hour traffic. As soon as Peter got in the car, I blurted it out, expecting him to be as shocked as I was. But he was very calm.

'I said "You don't even seem surprised," and he said "I'm not really. I've been worried it was something like this for a long time, but I didn't want to worry you."'

An appointment had been made for Karen and both parents at their local children's hospital. There they saw a doctor who told them that Karen was developing 'at half speed'.

Sue: 'That didn't seem so bad; it means that at 26 months she was functioning like a 13-month old. Two months later, we were seen by a consultant paediatrician and that's when we got the really bad news. He told us that she would be very seriously handicapped and that she was autistic, a condition I'd never even heard of.

'The news hit us both very badly, but Peter was the strong one. I'm fortunate in that. I know of other families where the husband just couldn't cope and I dread to think what would have happened if Peter had been like that, because without his support I couldn't have got through the next year.

'I went through a very bad patch. I'd cry everytime I saw a baby. I had an absolute thing about little girls Karen's age. I'd go to the park and watch them running around. Then I'd look at Karen and feel so bitter and cheated. The doctor put me on anti-depressants, but they just made me sleep. Peter finally said "Enough is enough. This is no good. You're impossible to live with and you're not helping Karen." He didn't put his arm around me and say, "There, there." He was quite firm, and for me this worked. I started to see sense and pulled myself out of the depression.

'We took Karen to hospital for routine assessments and every time they saw her she seemed to have got worse. I don't believe she is autistic, but at first she certainly behaved that way. She'd sit in a corner, rocking and making repetitive sounds all day. She was very withdrawn and wouldn't let you cuddle or touch her. Then, when she was around 5 years of age, the autism seemed to disappear.

'Till she was 8 she walked around the house quite well, though she wouldn't walk outside. In fact she'd walk up and down the hall so much, we reckoned she must have covered about 10 miles a day! Something happened as she got bigger though. Her mobility decreased. She didn't want to walk and we had to get her a buggy. Now she's in a wheelchair, which is very frustrating when you know she could walk at least a little. Last year she had to have an operation on her tendons because she couldn't put her feet flat on the ground. She has lost the use of her legs because she doesn't want to use them. It's difficult to understand.

'Now, when she's not at school, Karen just sits in her chair and stares into space. She doesn't enjoy food; I often think that if I didn't feed her she wouldn't care. You push the food into her mouth and she lets it fall out. I suspect she doesn't see the purpose of the whole messy business.'

Once she began to come to terms with Karen's disability, Sue says, she wanted to have another baby. Her husband, Peter, wasn't so sure.

Sue: 'He worried that we might have another like Karen. I worried too but I wanted a baby so badly I was prepared to put it out of my mind.

'We discussed it with our doctor and he felt Karen's condition was just one of those things. We'll probably never know exactly why she is as she is. Of course we went round the family trying to find out if there was anyone else with mental problems, even distant relations. We didn't find anyone.

'Peter was worried too about the coping side of things – me looking after two helpless babies really. But in the end he said as long as I was sure. I wanted a girl. I didn't analyse that and I don't think I'd have been too disappointed if I'd had a boy, as long as it was a normal child, doing normal things.

'From the day the pregnancy was confirmed everything seemed all right. I was my old-self again. Any trace of worry that something would go wrong disappeared and it made me accept Karen's handicap much better. I can't explain it; it's just how it was. It wasn't until after Tracey was born that I realized it hadn't been like this for Peter. He'd been under a great strain during the pregnancy, worrying all the time. But once he'd seen her, he relaxed. Because Karen's problems hadn't been noticed until quite late, I suppose we watched Tracey with a bit more than the usual anxiety, but she was such a forward baby it was obvious she was okay.

'The next few years were hard, with three young children, but it could have been harder if Karen had been a difficult child. As it was she could be popped into her chair while I changed the baby. She wouldn't run away or anything and she didn't demand attention constantly. She's time-consuming, but not demanding.

'We told Joe, our eldest, about Karen's handicap soon after we had the diagnosis. But he was only 4½; what he understood was limited. He just accepted her. The fact that she's not difficult and never did anything embarrassing in front of his friends was a great help. She's never interfered with his life. We could still lead a normal family life, more or less. We've always been able to take Karen out for a meal with us. She'd never make a scene, just sit there quiet as a lamb.

'Of course I had to feed her and people would sometimes stare, but Joe never took any notice. Tracey now is different. Even when she was as young as 5, she hated people looking. She'd say "What's up with them? Haven't they ever seen a handicapped child?" She's always been very adult and headstrong, an amazingly independent little girl. I sometimes worry that she grew up too soon, but it wasn't that I forced her. She wanted to feed herself as soon as she could get hold of a spoon. She was out of nappies at 20 months.'

Sue works as a classroom assistant, a job she has had for 8 years, and loves.

Sue: 'It's a dream of a job that fits in with family life. I'd hate to have to give it up – it's not just the money, but the social side, getting out of the house. You need that badly with a child like Karen. At the moment things are fine. Karen can stay at her school till she is 19, but there is only one special care unit for adults in the city, and not nearly enough places to go round. The council is supposed to be opening another one soon, but I worry that it will fill up before Karen gets there, and I'll have to give up work and have her at home all day.

'There are always problems. It's the same with respite care. We use a shared care scheme, run by the council, where Karen goes to a host family for up to 6 weeks a year. It's been absolutely life-saving for us. We use it for the summer holiday, odd weekends and overnight stays. We know our host family very well and think a lot of them. But the couple's own three daughters are grown up and now they have no ties, they are thinking of giving up this work and travelling. I can't imagine how we'll find another suitable family to take Karen at her age.

'Having Karen could have split me and Peter up or pulled us together. Fortunately it did the latter. It made us grow up very quickly. We were married when I was 19; I had my first baby at 20 and we are both "only children", quite protected from the hard knocks. Then in the year I was expecting Karen I lost my father, who'd idolized me, and when Karen was 4 weeks old Peter's mum died. We had two very rough years and we had very few people to turn to, not having brothers and sisters, so we clung together. Gradually we realized that Karen's handicap wasn't the end of the world. There were other things in life.

'These last 2 years though I feel I've been going through another phase in my life. My son is grown up, Tracey is no longer a little girl. Our friends with children of the same age are now free to spend time together, to go out in the evenings without worrying about a baby sitter. And it's suddenly hit me that as long as Karen is here, I'll never have that freedom.

'I've sat here alone with Karen and thought "This is how it is always going to be." It terrifies me. I knew it before of course, but now I *feel* it too. I love her dearly, but I feel so very trapped.'

BRIAN

Eighteen-year-old Brian is the youngest of three boys. His father, Joe, works as a driver. Maureen, his mother, is a full-time housewife, but much of her spare time is taken up with voluntary work for people with mental handicap locally. They live in a small industrial town.

Maureen: 'The trouble is Brian doesn't fit in at school. There's a lot he can do; he feeds himself, he tells us when he wants to go to the toilet, though they don't believe this at school. They take him every hour and claim he's only clean and dry by chance. Once they sent him home in a nappy and I hit the roof.

'They put him in special care, where the others – and I'm not saying it's their fault – can't do anything. He gets so bored he bites his shirt and does silly things. He should be in the main school. He's better with children more able than himself.

'I keep fighting and shouting and carrying on, but nothing gets done. He seems to be a forgotten child. He only started getting speech therapy recently because I accidentally met a speech therapist who goes into the school and she thought Brian would benefit. The school had never suggested she see him. I've no idea what Brian does at school all day. The headmaster won't allow parents in without an appointment – which is the only way you'd get a realistic view of what goes on.

'There's not much point in fighting now. He'll be at the adult training centre soon. I just hope he fits in better there – he's been the square peg in the round hole for too long.'

Maureen says Brian seemed a normal baby till he was 6 months old and started routine childhood inoculations.

Maureen: 'He had the first triple injection just before we went on holiday and he cried all the way to Devon. We took him to the hospital when we got home and they said there was nothing wrong but they'd keep an eye on him. My husband thinks it was the injection that caused all Brian's problems, but I'm not sure, and anyway you couldn't prove it.

'He developed very slowly. He didn't sit up till he was nearly 12 months and I suppose I should have known, especially having had two other babies. But you fool yourself, don't you? Relatives would say he should be doing this and that and I'd say he was slow because he was such a heavy baby, that's all. He was over 9lbs when he was born.

'By this time we were attending a clinic at the hospital. There was an occupational therapist there, a nasty piece of work. One day she said to me: "He'll never do anything, you know. You should put him away and forget about him." I remember telling Joe, my husband, that evening and he broke down. It was the first time I'd ever seen him cry. The funny thing is I don't remember anybody ever telling us officially that Brian had a mental handicap. We were just absorbed into the system. It was accepted that we knew.

'I think Joe had more trouble accepting it than me. He seemed to think that if he ignored it, it would go away. Even now, if he tells anyone about Brian, he'll always add straight afterwards, "The other two are perfect." I always know it's coming. It amuses me.

'Brian's always been accepted as part of the family. The two older boys, Ray and Steven, idolize him. If he's not there when they come in they'll say, "Where's the babby? Is the little 'un not here?" It's the same with Ray's wife, though I think it took her a while to get used to. Steven, who's 21, has a steady girlfriend now and I can see she's not really at ease with Brian yet. One of the things that worries people at first is the way he sits so close. He can't sit in a chair near you, he has to be almost on your lap.

'I think Brian understands a lot. He talks with his eyes. The other day Steven was going out with his girlfriend and my daughter-in-law, who was visiting, said "That's another one who'll be leaving you soon, Brian." He looked so sad; you could see that's what he was thinking. He does miss them. He came away on holiday with just his dad and me for the first time this year and he was miserable and disruptive. It was a nightmare. Steven said, "I don't blame him. I wouldn't want to go away with two old fogies either!"

'I have to admit I'm dreading Steven leaving home. There was a spell when he was at college, Ray had left home and my husband was away all the time driving a tanker, and I just couldn't cope. It isn't that they actually look after Brian much but having someone around, some company, makes it that much easier. What really hurt was that Joe couldn't understand this. He couldn't see what I was talking about.

'He did change his job though, so that he has regular working hours, and after a while Steven changed to a day-release course, so I was okay again. But it does worry me how I'll cope in the future.'

The family live in an area where a share-care system of respite care operates, with the natural family being paired with a host family who will look after the child for short periods. Brian goes away from Saturday evening till Sunday evening twice a month and a couple of days a week in the school holidays. Unusually his main carer is a man, who now has his girlfriend living at his house. Maureen is satisfied with this arrangement.

Maureen: 'You do need a break even if it's just to get a lie-in occasionally. Sometimes Brian can be very wearing. Like yesterday when I met a friend and took him shopping and he went berserk in Woolworths. He went red and started shaking and shouting and banging about. It came on suddenly and I had no idea what had set him off, though he sometimes gets excited when he's trying to tell you he wants to go to the toilet. We had to leave of course and rush him home as quickly as possible. By which time he'd calmed down and didn't want the toilet after all.

'It's at times like that I look at him and think, "Heaven help me – I can't live with you and I can't live without you."'

CHARLOTTE

Before she was born, Charlotte's parents were warned that there would be problems. Phillippa, her mother, says: 'It was quite scary. We didn't know what to expect. The doctors didn't tell us the details and I'm not sure how much they knew anyway. Alec, my husband, was told that if the only way the baby could survive was on a life support machine, he would have to decide whether or not the machine should be switched off – a terrible decision, which, fortunately, he didn't have to make.'

Charlotte was born with hydrocephalus, which caused brain damage. She is now 16 and an only child. Her father is a senior manager in the health service.

Phillippa: 'She was much more handicapped than I'd imagined. The size of her head was very obvious. I had a bad time trying to cope when I took her home. No matter how supportive a husband is, it's the mother who has to take the responsibility. If I'd started thinking, at that stage, on the level of feeling cheated, or comparing Charlotte to normal babies, I'd have gone to pieces, so I concentrated on the practical things. I'm quite good at suppressing feelings and not facing up to facts! But I was aware of the terrible isolation, of feeling like the only person in the world with a child like Charlotte. The only help I had came from my mother and a district nurse who used to call in.

'It didn't help that my husband was unable to talk about it. Even now when there are problems concerning our daughter that need sorting out, he shies away from them. I just get a yes or no to my questions. I don't know why. It's meeting other mums, being involved in coffee mornings and the school support group that has eased my isolation. I can talk to them about Charlotte and be sure they are interested and understanding.

'We wanted four children when we got married, but time passed and I had difficulty conceiving. I was in my thirties and halfway through adopting when I found I was pregnant. We cancelled the adoption. I knew the likelihood of me having a second child was remote and it never happened. It didn't particularly bother me; Charlotte took up all my time anyway. When she went to school at 3½, I was relieved at not having to cope with her all day, but at the same time I was desperately upset at being apart from her for hours on end – very confusing.

'She's happy at school. When she leaves I expect she will go to an adult centre. There's one 2 minutes walk from us, but it's full. You have to trust there will be vacancies or a new one in 2 years' time. I'd rather she wasn't in a special care unit and her headteacher feels that with some ancillary care she could cope in an ordinary centre. She can walk if you hold her hands, though she has some spasticity; and she can take herself to the toilet or tell you she wants to go, if she is in her usual environment. If we go away though I always take a plastic sheet

'Charlotte can talk, and though a lot of what she says comes from nursery rhymes or songs, it's often appropriate. But she repeats things over and over too, like "grandad's house" or "where are we going?" You can answer the question but she'll still keep repeating it. She was assessed as two-thirds behind normal, so her mental age is about 5.'

Charlotte stays with a local family for respite care, going there straight from school, staying overnight and returning home after school next day. The present respite carers are the fourth the family have had and Phillippa admits to having had reservations when she first began to use the service.

Phillippa: 'You think that no one else can do things properly for her and that they won't love her. I've liked most of the families, though there was one lady I wasn't particularly happy with. It's hard to be objective when meeting them and a lot of your fears are based on snobbishness if you are honest with yourself. All you're objecting to is that the people are from a different background to you.'

Phillippa admits to marital disharmony, though she is not certain how much of this can be attributed to Charlotte's disability and how much to the natural wear and tear of married life.

Phillippa: 'All I can say is that Alec and I were very close before she was born and now we hardly talk or share anything. I've recently come through a depression caused partly by the terrible resentment I feel, much of it directed at Alec, rightly or wrongly.

'I don't blame him – or myself for that matter – for Charlotte's handicaps. I don't suffer from that kind of guilt. But I do resent the fact that I don't get more support and that I am not able to talk to him. If I could talk, I could let off steam and not have to bottle it up.

'There are issues that need to be talked out, such as Charlotte's future. One day she will have to live in residential care. I'd like her to live in a small unit in an ordinary road, and I'd like to see her settled while she's young and flexible, before we are old. But I can't get Alec to discuss it and I don't feel like taking the entire responsibility myself. Why should I shoulder it alone?

'I appreciate the friendships I've made with other mothers through Charlotte, but I just feel I've reached a stage in my life where I want to be something in addition to the mother of a child with a mental handicap. I want to be myself.'

FAREY

Farey lies on her back in bed under a pretty, floral quilt. Her eyes are closed. When her mother, Sahira, touches her face and calls her, she opens them reluctantly for a moment but makes no eye contact. She is 15, small and fragile. She eats only liquidized food and little of that. Sahira, who came from Pakistan to marry her husband, spends hours feeding her, and anxious nights, when Farey is wakeful and crying, trying to work out what is hurting her.

Farey is doubly incontinent, cannot sit or hold anything and functions on the level of a small baby. Her bed doesn't need a cot side because she cannot move enough to fall out. On a bedside cabinet are the 6 bottles of medicine she has to be given daily. This is the second child with severe mental and physical handicaps born to the family. Their first disabled child, also a daughter, died 8 years ago at the age of 10. There are two healthy sons, aged 14 and 17. The girls' condition was established as genetic after Farey's birth. When she became pregant with her younger son, Sahira was offered an abortion.

Sahira: 'I got pregnant accidentally. My doctor says "no more babies", but once I was pregnant I decided to make this baby. I was very frightened, but I could not have an abortion. It would not have been right. When my son was born, my family said straight away that he was alright, but I couldn't believe it – not for a few hours, until I could see for myself that he was clenching his fists and crying and moving like a healthy baby. Then I relaxed and was happy.'

It was her mother-in-law who noticed, soon after the birth, that the first baby had problems.

Sahira: 'I noticed nothing. To me she was just beautiful. We called her Dolly, a pet name. But my mother-in-law was worried and said that both of her legs looked blue. I knew nothing about babies, so my mother-in-law asked the doctor. The doctor gave the baby an injection and told us she would be all right, she was just cold.

'I didn't know what to think. We took her home and we kept watching and hoping, but she never did any of the things a baby should. Then when she was 3 months old, she started to have fits. In hospital they did tests and told us she would not be a normal child. We all felt very, very sad; my husband and me, my in-laws and my parents in Pakistan. But still I kept hoping that she might not be too bad.

'She was like Farey, but not so handicapped. She could say some words, and she understood a lot. She could enjoy certain things, and she loved my husband's parents so much. Too much maybe – we could never leave her with anyone else.'

When Dolly was ten, her fits became very severe. She was kept in hospital for a couple of months, then discharged, without explanation. She died, suddenly, sitting on her mother's lap, as she tried to feed her.

Sahira: 'She just fell forward and stopped breathing. I couldn't believe it . . . I didn't want to believe it. My father-in-law was in the house and he picked her up, but she was dead. Afterwards we found out that the staff at the hospital knew she was going to die. But they never told us and they should have. We could have been prepared. People said "You have another daughter and two sons, it's for the best, forget about her," but I can never ever forget. Dolly was special; nobody can take her place.'

The birth of the second, normal child gave her and her husband the confidence to have more.

Sahira: 'But when Farey was born, I knew straight away she was not all right. She looked just like her sister, and at 5 days old she started shaking. It was the start of her fits. They kept her in the special care baby unit for 3 months, but there was nothing they could do. After that we had blood tests and they told us that if we had more children there was a risk of them being born with these handicaps. We accept that it is something in the family.

'My sister, who was living in Kuwait, also had a handicapped son, her first child. I was so worried when she had her other children, in case it would happen as with us, but, you see, her other children are normal. No one else in our families have ever had children like this. Until I came to England I had never seen children with handicaps but maybe that is because in Pakistan we do not have such good hospitals and children who are not healthy die.'

During the years when she had two children with severe multiple disabilities to care for, Sahira acknowledges that her life was very difficult.

Sahira: 'It was hard for me to get out of the house, but my friends visited me. They still do; Farey is not a big problem – everybody loves her. She goes to school in the minibus and the people there, the teachers and physiotherapist, try to help her. I have a very good social worker – she doesn't come only if I have a problem; she calls to see me regularly and she gets me lots of help. I have a special chair shaped to fit Fairey so that she doesn't have to lie down all the time. My social worker arranged for a family who will have her during the day if I have to go out. Or there is a sitter who will come into the house and look after Farey here.

'When I went to Pakistan to see my mother, my husband and sons looked after her at night and at the weekend. A sitter came in the mornings to get her ready for school and in the afternoons to look after her till my husband got home. She has never been away overnight. We wouldn't want that, I think she will always live with us at home.

'Children like Farey are special. Your other children may do bad things, cause problems. But these children will never harm anyone; they will never hurt you.'

Strictly speaking this is a book about families who have kept their son or daughter with a mental handicap at home; the following two case histories are the exceptions. Both Michael and Jackie now live away from home and their mothers talk – in very different terms – about the circumstances which led the families to make this choice.

Ellen, Michael's mother, lives in a small industrial town in the Midlands; Pam and her husband come from a city in the south-west.

MICHAEL

Ellen, a part-time secretary, and her husband, John, have two sons, 11-year-old Alan and 14-year-old Michael. Michael has a mental handicap and challenging behaviour. He attends a residential school 120 miles from his family. They speak to him on the telephone and visit him every 6 weeks, but Ellen says she would never have him living at home again.

Ellen: 'Michael went away when he was 6 – not to the place he's at now, but to a local hospital unit. It was meant to be just a short stay of about 6 weeks to give us a break, but in that time we found out what life could be like without him and we just couldn't go back to the way things were.

'Don't think it was an easy decision. I was in turmoil over whether we were doing the right thing. I felt we were sacrificing Michael for the sake of the rest of the family. The place he was staying in wasn't even suitable – he was with much older boys – and I was aware there was a lot of criticism behind my back from other mothers.

'Even the professionals would tell us that Michael would be far better off at home. I couldn't disagree with them, but if he'd stayed with us any longer there wouldn't have been a home.

'I don't think anyone who hasn't lived with a child like Michael could understand what we went through during those 6 years. There was always the possibility that my husband might walk out, but towards the end I was the one on the point of leaving. And I would have if a place hadn't been found for Michael.'

There was no hint of the problems to come when Michael was born.

Ellen: 'I took home a completely normal child as far as I was concerned. I didn't know much about how babies were meant to develop, but as I kept in touch with two other mothers I met in the maternity hospital I was able to compare notes and Michael was definitely not an easy baby.

'He slept very little – at 5 weeks he could stay awake all night. At 4 months, he suddenly started to go stiff after feeds, like a little fit, but the staff at the clinic said it was just one of those things. It stopped at 7 months. When he was 12 months old and way behind the babies of my friends, someone finally took some notice and decided it was time to do some tests. The results were all normal – and we were back to being told that I was an over-anxious mother. At 18 months, when he still wasn't walking, I was meeting people who were saying, "Don't worry, mine didn't walk till he was 2 and he's fine."

'I don't know if this attitude was something to do with the fact that we lived in Liverpool where they are very child-orientated. All babies are wonderful to them. When I was expecting my second – knowing, by this time, that Michael was handicapped – people were shocked when I told them I was having tests and would have an abortion if there was anything wrong. They tried to persuade me I couldn't possibly have an abortion, but of course I would have done, at whatever stage it was known there was a problem. I still feel it would have been better if we'd known about Michael and he hadn't been born.'

At a routine appointment when Michael was 26 months old, a doctor broke the news to Ellen and her husband that he had a mental handicap.

Ellen: 'He wasn't exactly telling us anything we didn't know, but it is still shattering to have your worst fears confirmed. It was especially so because around that time Michael had put on a spurt and was starting to do things, and we were beginning to lull ourselves into thinking he was just a slow developer. I suppose I thought in terms of "He'll grow up to be a milkman instead of a scientist."

'He looked so normal, you see, like an angel — and suddenly there was this terrible label "mentally handicapped" hanging over us. The only relief for me was knowing that it wasn't something I was doing that was holding him back, and that I wasn't a neurotic mother. Up until then that's the impression I'd been given.

'We don't know what caused the problem — probably something that happened in pregnancy they say. I racked my brains for anything significant. All I could think of was a time, very early on when I didn't know I was pregnant, and I drank a lot and got tiddly. But I don't suppose that could have caused it really.

'I had thought about the possibility of having a child with a handicap during pregnancy because of my age — I was 33. I remember saying quite determinedly that if I had a Down's Syndrome baby I would not take it out of the hospital. Ironic really that I got tricked into thinking I had a normal baby. I very much wish I'd known at the beginning and that Michael could have gone into care when he was younger. Those few years at home didn't make any difference to him. I'd have had a third child if he hadn't been at home and I regret missing out on that, on a brother or sister for Alan.

'It is hard to describe what life was like with Michael once he was up and walking. He never stopped. I simply couldn't take my eyes off him for a minute. I couldn't go to the toilet without taking him with me and trying to hang on to his hand. My husband had no life either. When he walked in from work he got the kids thrown at him because I couldn't take it a minute longer.

'Michael was totally uncontrollable and the more angry you became, the more you shouted or smacked him, the more he enjoyed it. He'd just laugh. He never reacted normally. I'm surprised now that one of us didn't harm him. We often reached the pitch where we might have, but fortunately, not at the same time. One of us would always restrain the other.

'I was frightened of breaking his arm because he used to fight me when I tried to dress him and I'd have to force his limbs into clothes. I couldn't control him in any manner or way. And it was even worse when Alan arrived. Everyone said "Have another child, it will help Michael." Nobody said Michael would make life a nightmare for the other child, which is what happened.

'Alan never got a look in. I totally neglected him for 3 years. Every time I'd start to do something with him, Michael would do something and I'd have to leave Alan. He quickly learned that the only way to get my attention was by being naughty. He also learned to copy Michael. When a new health visitor arrived for the first time, she told me afterwards, she had no idea by looking at them which of my children had the handicap. They were both tearing around behaving bizarrely.

'It was this health visitor who fought for a residential place for Michael. She could see what was happening to the family, that it was on the brink of breaking down. At that stage I'd have been satisfied with weekend care, but we couldn't get it, so we stuck out for a full-time placement. It's a pity you can't ask for this sort of thing rationally; that you have to virtually threaten to kill the child to get taken seriously. We lasted about a month after we asked them to find a place, with the health visitor coming in every day because she was so concerned about us.

'For a long time after Michael went away I felt guilty and very inadequate. I felt I should have been able to cope; other people could. Then they tried to place Michael with a foster family, people experienced with difficult children, and they only kept him for a day. I didn't feel so bad after that.

'He's in his present place basically because the original unit was being moved into the community and couldn't cope with him out of purpose-built accommodation. We are very happy with the school. There are 3 staff to every child and they are very experienced. If he'd gone somewhere like this years ago he might be a different boy now. There has been discussion about him coming back home when he is too old for the school but we've said no. We won't contemplate it. It's only in the last few years that I've manage to free myself from the worry and the guilt and actually started to live a normal life, the kind of life most of the population take for granted. I'm not prepared to give that up.'

JACKIE

'She's a beautiful, warm, loving girl,' Pam says of her 19-year-old daughter. 'She loves people and people say she's a joy to know.' But there is another side to Pam's only child. Jackie's behaviour can be difficult and by the time she was 16 she was becoming too much for both parents and her school to handle.

Jackie now attends a residential school, coming home for holidays. Her parents visit her once a month. Pam is a school teacher.

Pam: 'We didn't want her to go away, but the problem is she's so strong. The staff at school were frightened to take her out because she was liable to run into the road and drag one of the care assistants with her under the wheels of a bus. If you let go of her hand, she'd just run.

'I was feeling the strain too. Every time I went into the school the headteacher would look at me and say, "Oh dear, she really is getting too much for you." The teachers also felt that if Jackie could be somewhere where there was a constant 24-hour regime, her behaviour would improve. Her father and I began to think that if everyone was saying this, maybe we ought to give it a try.

'Oh, but we did miss her when she went. I felt absolutely lost. People say, "You must dread the holidays," but I love having her home. Even when she pulls my hair and fastens her fingers round wrought iron gates and refuses to budge when we're out walking. Even though we have to lock all the doors so she won't run away and lock everything breakable out of sight. But I have to admit she'd be too much for me on a permanent basis now."'

Pam wanted more children, but Jackie's condition is genetic ('If I'd had a second one the same, I'd have jumped off the suspension bridge with one in each arm!') She suffers from an enzyme deficiency, which was diagnosed, following a series of fits, at 2½.

Pam: 'It was the fourth fit she'd had – the doctor hadn't taken much notice of the earlier ones – and it was massive. It went on for hours and hours. She was taken into hospital and that's when we found out about the enzyme deficiency. They also told us that she probably wouldn't live beyond the age of 3, though she might, possibly, survive till she was 8. The prognosis was that she would go into a fit and not come out of it.

'As you can imagine, it was absolutely devastating news. Her brain had been damaged by the fit. She couldn't walk, couldn't even sit up, and though she had been clean and dry before, she was now incontinent. But none of this mattered. We just wanted our little girl alive, whatever. We'd have done anything to keep her. I was absolutely determined I wasn't goint to let her die.

'A friend of mine suggested, tentatively, that I should try a spiritual healer she'd been to. She said she didn't normally tell people this because they might think her a bit strange. Well, I didn't care what anyone thought. I made an appointment, trying not to pin my hopes on it.

'The healer put her hands on Jackie's head and said yes, she'd suffered severe brain damage and it wasn't possible to make any promises, but she'd like to see her again. It was on the third visit that she told me I needn't worry; Jackie wasn't going to die.

'After that, Jackie had three very tiny fits and then nothing, not for a very long time. The hospital doctors said they could see an improvement but couldn't account for it. I still worried, of course, especially when she was around 3 years old. I used to have nightmares in which little coffins floated past me. After I'd put her to bed at night, I was upstairs every ten minutes checking she was alright.'

Gradually Jackie regained many of the skills she had lost, but she was left with severe learning difficulties and behaviour patterns which have been diagnosed as autistic.

Pam: 'She has certain little autisms. She'll always have to touch the ground when she sits down and she will push crockery, bit by bit, to the very edge of a table. But if autistic children are withdrawn, that's certainly not my daughter. She understands a great deal but she doesn't communicate verbally in the sense of holding a conversation. She repeats things and says "No" forcefully if she doesn't want to do something.

'Once we began to believe that she was going to live, James, my husband, and I settled into a routine. When one of us was exhausted, the other would take over. We have coped and were glad to have her here to cope with, though there were times when we could have done with the support of a social worker. But if they know you're coping, they leave you to get on with it, don't they? The only time James and I have fallen out is over discipline. When Jackie is difficult, he believes in smacking her; I don't. The last time she was home from school, we had a disagreement in a restaurant. He didn't like the way she was behaving so he smacked her. And I shouted, "Don't you do that. You can't smack a 19-year-old. She is a young woman."

'I know I should always treat her the same and be totally consistent, but I'm human. A lot depends on how you feel. She used to wander down at night when she was supposed to be in bed. Sometimes I'd take her back straight away and tell her to stay there, very firmly; other times I'd let her stay down, and play with her.'

Jackie's first residential school closed down and after a short spell at home she moved to the one she now attends. On her third day there, she had a fit, her first for 13 years, and was taken to hospital in a coma. Pam's first thought was to call the spiritual healer, who went with her to the hospital.

Pam: 'I slept on a camp bed beside Jackie for 2 weeks. The doctors didn't hold out much hope for her but gradually she came out of the coma. She came home to recuperate and when we took her back to the school, for the first time she didn't want to let us go. She's normally very adaptable, very happy to be with new people, but she hung on to our hands. She soon settled though, and she's been fine; no fits. They think the last one was the result of a stray virus which sent her temperature rocketing.'

Pam has worked since Jackie was a toddler.

Pam: 'Initially I helped out at a nursery school three mornings a week and Jackie came along as a pupil. Then I worked part-time when she started at the special school. It wasn't until she went away that I realized what stress I'd worked under. I'd get to the school just in time for my lessons and leave immediately afterwards. Suddenly I didn't have this permanent ticking clock tied to me. I had all the time in the world. I could get in early and stay around for a leisurely chat. I've also got involved with a voluntary group for people for people with mental handicap. I'm secretary.'

Pam is very aware that another crisis looms ahead, for Jackie will soon have to leave her school.

Pam: 'I'm hoping, praying, that she'll be accepted by Home Farm Trust for one of their residential homes, but they haven't made up their minds yet. They may decide she's too much of a problem. Heaven only knows where she'll go if that happens. Home, I suppose. Sometimes I feel guilty about sending her away. Then I remind myself that it's common sense to get her settled while we're able. And I know what would happen if she was at home. She'd get bored and frustrated – and then she'd start pulling my hair out.'

GETTING HELP

Association of Crossroads Care Attendant Schemes

For information on home care and sitting service schemes nationally.

10 Regent Place,
Rugby,
Warwickshire CV21 2PN.
Tel: 0788 73653.

Gateway Clubs

Around 700 leisure clubs in England, Wales and Northern Ireland for teenagers and adults with a mental handicap. They provide everything from dancing and sport to holidays and outings.

National Federation of Gateway Clubs,
MENCAP,
123 Golden Lane,
London EC1Y 0RT.
Tel: 071 454 0454.

Independent Living Fund

Discretionary charitable trust which helps people with severe handicaps to stay at home by contributing towards the cost of help – i.e. care attendants, domestic help. The claim has to come from the disabled person, but parents can claim on his/her behalf. Claimant must be 16 or over and receiving Attendance Allowance.

The Independent Living Fund,
P.O. Box 183,
Nottingham NG8 3RD.
Tel: 0602 290423.

Mobility Allowance

Cash benefit for people with severe disability who cannot, or can barely, walk. Available from the age of 5. Also acts as passport to Orange Badge Parking Scheme and free road tax. Ask for leaflet N1211 at your local Social Security office. *

Motability

Helps disabled people who want to use their mobility allowance to buy or lease a car. Under the hire purchase scheme it is possible to buy a new or used car, or an electric wheelchair.

Motability,
Gate House,
Westgate,
The High,
Harlow,
Essex CM20 1HR.
Tel: 0279 635666.

Severe Disablement Allowance

Weekly cash benefit for people aged 16 or over who are unable to work because of disability. Someone claiming SDA can usually claim *Income Support* to 'top up' allowance. Income Support also acts as passport to other benefits, such as free prescriptions and dental care. For information contact your local DSS office.

Transport

Door to Door is a guide to getting around which brings together basic information about transport for people with disabilities. This includes trains, boats and planes, but also Dial-a-Ride schemes and taxi care schemes. Free from:

Department of Transport,
Door to Door Guide,
Freepost,
South Ruislip,
Middlesex HA4 0NZ.

*When Attendance and Mobility Allowance combine to form the Disability Living Allowance, there will be a second lower rate Mobility Allowance, which should become available to many people with a mental handicap.

3 Young Adults

CHANGES

The late teens is a fairly fraught period for parents and child alike. It's the time when the teenager leaves the school which may have been a familiar and secure base since early childhood and moves to a Social Services day centre. There are other possible options at this stage, including full or part-time courses at local or residential colleges and sheltered or open employment, but the vast majority will go to a local day centre. (They used to be called adult training centres, but now go under a variety of names, the simplest and most self-explanatory being day centre.)

If parents felt confident that their son or daughter was going on to better things, they might be less anxious, but unfortunately day service staff-levels and facilities rarely match up to those left behind at school.

In some ways this is justified, on the grounds that these are adults who should not have their lives as tightly supervised and organized as children in schools. They have the right to more freedom and therefore do not need as high a ratio of staff. This is a worthy notion, and fine for the more able people, but is totally unrealistic for those with more severe handicaps, learning difficulties or behaviour problems.

Martin Gallagher, MENCAP divisional general manager, whose area stretches from Lands End to Staffordshire, gets more parental complaints about day services than any other facility – particularly about the shortfall of places, which can leave youngsters at home for 24 boring hours each day and parents tearing their hair out. Those already in centres may find their time cut to 2 or 3 days per week in order to offer a little time to new school leavers without a place, or they may be excluded for weeks becuse of staff shortages. The cause? Too little cash, due to the now-familiar cutbacks.

The staff make the best of a bad job, but often there are too few of them for the tasks demanded. A day care officer in the special care unit at my son's day centre grew positively starry-eyed talking about a week when two-thirds of her group were away on holiday.

It was wonderful being able to take the remaining ones out with plenty of helpers to give them the attention they needed. They really responded. Some started doing things they hadn't attempted before. It was so rewarding for us, and so unusual. Normally we have time for basic care – and that's not what the job should be about, nor what these people deserve.

Even if there's a smooth passage from school to a relatively good centre, parents are often shocked by the difference from their child's school. Some find the lack of involvement very disappointing. One mother complained:

It's so big and impersonal – there must be nearly 200 people here. It's a whole different atmosphere from school where there were less than 50 children. I never know what my son has been doing. They don't seem to consult parents when they are making changes or even tell them afterwards. The only time I hear from the centre is when they want me to sell raffle tickets or notify me of a disco – not my kind of thing, I'm afraid. What I'd like are organized parents' evenings where you can meet members of staff and discuss any problems about your child.

Add to this the fact that day services are currently in a state of flux, changing their ethos and their function and you'll see the potential for dissatisfaction and anxiety among parents and consumers. (The old terms 'clients' and 'students' are changing as well.) On the whole though, it wasn't the parents of young people just starting the centres who complained – most were grateful to have a place even if it was less then perfect – but the older parents whose sons or daughters had been there when different ideas prevailed (see Chapter 4).

These parents were unhappy about what they saw as a new style of professional managers, who they suspected of being inexperienced and unrealistic about people with a mental handicap. They are bitter about the way changes have taken place without consultation with them, but what they regret most is the passing of the day-centre-as-workplace. They yearn for the days when simple contract work used to be brought in and those who were capable would put in a day at the work bench for a very small wage. In many centres, with an eye to fairness, the money was split between those who worked and those who were too handicapped to, which made the sum even smaller.

Parents say the amount of cash wasn't important. What mattered to their son or daughter was the feeling that they were going to work like everyone else and receiving a pay packet at the end of the week. They were happy then, now they are bored.

The feeling among professionals is that the old system was little short of slave labour. They point out that the old name 'training centre' was a total misnomer, with the so-called students being taught nothing. They believe they are creating instead a service which gives their people education, dignity and choice and takes them out of a ghetto and into the community. In many areas the centre building will be a base from which the consumers will go out to recreational or educational activities. Some may not visit much at all, but will go straight to work. Hopes are high – unrealistically so, say parents – of finding paid employment for many people.

One psychologist assured me that in her area day centres would be closed and jobs found for all consumers, even those with quite severe multiple handicaps:

> We will try for ordinary paid employment for everyone initially, and when and if those avenues are exhausted we'll look at the possibility of sheltered workshops. Nobody will be excluded on the grounds of severity of handicap. We have quite a few successes with people with severe multiple learning difficulties.

It is the sort of conviction that makes parents snort with derision, and threaten to dump their severely handicapped offspring on the employment office steps with the challenge to fix them up with a good job.

Most professionals, however, are not quite so optimistic. There is general recognition that there exists a large group of people who will not be working or attending college classes but will continue to need a base where they can stay and be cared for for a good part of each day.

There's also an admission that some parents may find a new system worrying. The psychologist just mentioned explained:

> With a day centre parents know their son or daughter will be there every day for set hours. It's cut and dried and they can plan their day

around it. A job situation is less secure. What if they don't fit in or lose the job, or need to work odd hours? They may have to stay at home at certain times. Parents tend to opt for the guaranteed place, but in this situation you have to think whose needs you are actually catering for – and it's got to be the clients.

It's probably true to say that parents and consumers will adapt to the new ideas but it would speed this up if there was a regular communication between centre staff and parents/carers. IPPs (Individual Programme Planning meetings) should bring the two sides together, along with other relevant professionals like social workers, at least once a year to discuss aims for the young person for the next 12 months. Sadly, few parents had been invited to such meetings. Most hadn't heard of them.

Day care provision is an area that galvanizes parents into action. They are fuelled by a mixture of deperation and anger, as they realize that their child is about to leave school and there is no certainty whatsoever that there will be any provision to replace it. Avon Mental Handicap Action Group was born out of such a situation, when fifty parents got together to fight for more day care centre places.

Forming a committee, they uncovered some startling statistics. It wasn't only their child who would be left high and dry when the school gates closed behind them for the last time. 484 places were needed in the next 3 years, and they didn't exist. A determined campaign, supported by the local media, persuaded the council to turn its attention and its financial clout to the neglected area. Flushed with success the full force of parent power is now being directed towards providing respite care for adults with profound and multiple handicaps and improving facilities in existing day care centres. Many centres, they say, are under-staffed, over-crowded and badly maintained. They want very specific improvements and smaller centres with none catering for more than a maximum of 100 people. The group is proof, if it's needed, that if they have the energy, time and persistence, parents can get things done. But should they have to?

THE DAY CENTRE

The wheels of progress grind round slowly and the day centre where Sue R works as an assistant manager is typical of many, caught halfway between the old and the new. The centre provides for 204 people, aged 19-72, with varying degrees of handicap and learning difficulties. It is still officially called an adult training centre, and the people who attend described as clients. It is run by a manager, a deputy and two assistant managers. Beneath them is a team of day care officers and care assistants.

Sue has responsibility for special care and special needs, the first catering for people with profound multiple handicap, the latter for those with challenging behaviour. Special care has 20 clients, cared for by 2 day care officers (at times only one) and 4 care assistants. The full complement of staff is not necessarily there every day. Holidays and illness and members of staff taking courses can change the situation.

Sue, for example, is presently doing a 3-year course, working towards a social worker qualification, which takes her out of the centre two days each week. And, although there is a replacement for her now that she is an assistant manager, there wouldn't necessarily be if she was still a DYO, as she was when she began the course. 'Replacements are never the same as your own staff somehow. They seem to get swallowed up,' she says.

There are plans to split up the special care and special needs units and integrate their clients into other groups. Sue explains:

> The idea is that profoundly handicapped people will have extra stimulation from the more able. With special needs clients, there's a feeling that as it stands, all the most difficult cases are shoved in together and they are very demanding for staff to deal with. If there are only two of them to each group, perhaps they will take their lead from the majority and their behaviour will improve. We have a few people at the centre who can be very aggressive and really need a member of staff all to themselves.

As part of a project on her course, Sue has visited a centre where these two special units have already been integrated.

> I found a mixture of opinions. One member of staff thought it was wonderful and said, 'It's so much better for the very handicapped ones. They have something to watch and active people around them.' But another pointed to his newly-integrated special care clients and said, 'Look at them. They can't do anything. What am I

expected to do? It ruins the chance of me doing anything interesting with my group.'

In Sue's centre, as in most others, the trend is away from 'work', partly she says because it was seen as exploitation, but also because companies have more automation nowadays and don't need these simple, repetitive jobs done by hand.

Some of the older clients say they miss the time when they used to pack curlers or whatever, but staff who were here then say clients didn't particularly enjoy it at the time. It can be a strain finding other ways of occupying them. It's certainly not an easy option. We work on normalization principles. For instance, clients no longer make their Christmas cards. Well, it's hardly normal. How many people without learning difficulties send their friends cards they've made themselves?

A lot of clients go out to courses at a nearby college – and not just the very able people. Our special needs people used to be excluded but this year they too have been accepted. There are a variety of courses tailored to our people – basic literacy, horticulture, keep fit, needlework.

Although we have a hydrotherapy pool here, the only people who use it are those who can't readily get out to the ordinary swimming baths in the community. The others go swimming where the rest of the population do, the municipal swimming baths. It's part of leading a normal life.

A group of volunteers take clients out for leisure activites. We organize holidays – on a canal boat, in chalets in the forest, at Butlins, and there's a big holiday in the Isle of Wight. Parents pay but it's subsidized. The idea is to get people out of the building and into the community as much as possible, so that the centre is just a base. The manager says his happiest day will be when the centre is completely empty!

Despite this, there are still plenty of activities within the centre including popmobility (a variation of keepfit), sequence dancing, woodwork and needlework. All are by choice. Says Sue: 'The girls still like to make soft toys but it's not a case of churning them out by the dozen as in the old days, when there were few outside activities and little choice.'

Another innovation is involving the clients in running the centre. 'There is a clients' committee, on which elected representatives put forward ideas and changes they would like to see,' Sue explains. 'At the early meetings, there were complaints about the toilets and about meals being cold and there being nowhere to put your bag, and I thought, "Oh dear, this is going to be real trivia." But gradually I realized that these things are not trivial at all but a big part of their lives. It is important that there should be working locks on the toilet doors and that toilet paper shouldn't always be running out. We'd complain too if it was us.'

She is aware of the shortcomings of the centre

Ideally we need more staff. Who doesn't? Filling vacancies is such a slow process. When someone gives notice, we are not allowed to advertise till they have actually left. It takes ages for the applications to be processed and the interviews completed. Altogether the process takes 3 months.

It would help if there was a pool of supply staff as there is in education. So far we haven't had to exclude clients because of staff problems as other places have, but it's been difficult. I'd like to see more training for staff and better pay for care assistants, which can be practically a nursing job for those dealing with severely handicapped people. Improving training and staff conditions filters down to the clients. You get more dedicated, knowledgeable workers.

Like many other centres, they have too few vacancies to meet the demands of special school leavers plus a steady stream of people being discharged from hospital to live in the community. There is a new 30-place annex being built for clients already waiting, receiving some care in a health authority unit.

'The local authority is not unaware of the problem,' says Sue. 'We've had councillors in to see the place, but when we know they are coming everybody makes a special effort and they never see the place at its worst. It's instinctive, I suppose, but self-defeating.'

I wondered if Sue and her colleagues meet parents. 'Not really,' she admitted. 'Most clients get here by special transport or are able to travel in alone, so we only see the few parents who bring in their son or daughter themselves. And there's never time for long discussion with them because we are so busy.'

RESPITE CARE

There's another age-related hurdle to be crossed at this time too. At around 18, young people cease to be children as far as respite care facilities are concerned and the search is on for an acceptable adult alternative.

For all but the most severely handicapped, the choice is likely to be between hostels (which, typically, have a few short-term beds among the full-time residents), family placement (similar to the shared care schemes for children, but rarer), hospital-based units or homes run by voluntary organizations. With the latter parents may have to pay, sometimes at a subsidized rate, or local authorities may foot the bill if they have nothing suitable to offer themselves. Sometimes, by necessity, they have to place someone in a home outside their own area. Frequently, of course, there is no choice for your particular child in your particular area; you take what is available.

Again, the biggest problems face those families whose child has profound, multiple handicaps or difficult behaviour. There are major cities and rich boroughs which simply have no respite care facilities, with round-the-clock staff and other expensive amenities required to care properly for these people.

Unless there's a hospital unit taking the most handicapped, or a voluntary organization offering some help (the Birmingham Multi-Handicap Group, for example, can provide carers to come into the home on a rota for periods up to a couple of weeks while the family is away) short-term breaks can become a thing of the past.

Some people feel that when the government's community care programme comes into effect, small private homes offering such care may mushroom. But as yet there's no evidence of this, or indeed what the quality of care might be if it happens.

That said, many parents of adults were tolerably happy with the respite care they had. In fact most lived in fear that it might be withdrawn, or changed beyond recognition to suit current trends rather than the individual. One mother, whose son is known for bouts of difficult behaviour, is horrified to hear that the modern hospital-based unit where he spends every weekend is to close.

They say that hospital is not the place for people like Adrian and they hope to get a house in the community instead. But he loves wandering around the hospital grounds. He's very active and needs the space. He'll be terribly restricted in a house with just an ordinary garden. That's the problem we have with him at home – he gets frustrated by being hemmed in. We're also worried that they'll close the hospital unit and then find there isn't enough money to run one in the community.

For many parents it's a case of what's available being better than nothing. 'The hostel my daughter goes to is not exactly what I'd choose,' one mother admitted. 'But you have to weigh up the needs. We need a rest and a bit of freedom and a week or a weekend there won't kill her.'

Another, whose daughter is just coming up to the cut-off age for the children's unit where she's been staying regularly for 10 years, says:

I'm terrified of trying to get her used to a new place. I'd say it took me a couple of years before she was happy in the place she's at now. She used to scream and cry. When we put her suitcase into the car to take her she'd say 'No holiday, no holiday,' because we used to say she was going on holiday to try to make it exciting. But we persevered and now she loves the place. She runs in when we stop the car outside. But can you imagine having to go through that all over again with a new place? In fact, I'm not sure I can face it. It might be easier just to keep her at home.

This was not the view of most parents of young adults, however. Many had evolved a settled pattern of which respite care and day care, however imperfect, were mainstays. Remove either, they said, and they weren't at all sure they could go on coping.

RELATIONSHIPS

Sexual relationships can be a worry to parents of teenagers and young adults. It's also an area where parents and professionals take widely opposite views. Many parents – the majority I spoke to, in fact – insist that their child has no interest in sex, and object strongly when people 'put ideas into their heads' by introducing the subject at day centres or in the later years at school.

Most professionals, however, see sexuality as a human right of which people with a mental handicap should not be deprived. So parents, when they mention the subject at all, talk of sexual problems, while professionals talk of sexual needs. Ann Craft, who lectures and writes widely on the subject, believes that sex education should be on the curriculum of all schools for children with learning difficulties and day centres. 'Sexual needs, feelings and drives are an inherent part of being human. They are not optional extras that we, in our wisdom, can choose to bestow or withhold according to whether someone passes an intelligence test.'

But sex education is only part of it. The forming of relationships, which can faze even those with the highest IQs, has to be learned. Says Sue R, assistant manager of a day centre:

> We are thinking of starting relationship groups at the centre to help our people over the initial hurdle of getting close to someone. Most of them have no idea how to make the first approach, but there are some very able people here, and some do form sexual relationships. I've never come across a couple doing anything more than cuddling, but others have, and they have to be told firmly that it's not acceptable. It is understandable though, because this is probably the only place they can be together.
>
> Most parents will not accept that their son or, in particular, their daughter, has a relationship. They deny that their children have such feelings. They want to go on seeing them as children. We have a very able Down's girl who has a boyfriend. We were on holiday from the centre and some of the parents came along, including the girl's mother. She wouldn't even let them hold hands, and it's very sad because this girl is bright and presentable. There's absolutely no reason why she shouldn't get married.

Psychologists working with people with learning difficulties regard only inappropriate sexual behaviour as a problem. This can involve another person but is more likely to be a solitary occupation, such as masturbating in public, in which case the aim would be to teach them what is an appropriately private place for such activity. Psychologist Sheila Jupp says: 'Sometimes excessive masturbation is the result of sheer boredom. If you can increase other activities it will reduce.'

Most parents would probably be relieved if it stopped completely, but Judith, mother of Simon, a strapping young man in his twenties, relies on her 'house rules':

> Fortunately, Simon understands everything he's told so he has no trouble grasping the rules. He is allowed to touch himself in bed, in the bath or in the bog – the three B's to make it simple – and absolutely nowhere else. He did start it on a bus once on the way to a museum. I whisked him straight off and on to a bus going in the opposite direction, home. He was very unhappy because the outing to the museum was a special treat, but he learned his lesson. He's never done it since.

Pauline Fairbrother, vice chair of MENCAP, is one parent who has no qualms about accepting her daughter's sexuality. For twenty-five years she has been trying to raise parental consciousness on the subject:

> When I started giving talks to parents I used to refer to 'sexual problems'. Then I realized that it was us, the parents, who had the problems – our children have sexual needs. In the early days it was difficult to even get my audience to look at me. It was very much a taboo subject, but over the years many people have come round to my way of thinking. Younger parents anyway are more willing to accept that their children will grow up to be sexual beings.
>
> Parents often ask what's the point of putting ideas into their children's heads, but the ideas are there already – as they are with all of us – in their bodies if not their heads. Denying it won't make it go away.

Pauline says that it was observing her daughter, Diana, the middle one of three girls, which brought the problems home to her.

> Di developed severe behaviour problems. She would smash things, attack people and make homelife hell for her sisters. It was obvious to me that this was part of adolescence and caused by frustration. My other two daughters also had their adolescent moods but they didn't go round smashing the place up because they had other outlets. Diana hadn't and she didn't understand what was happening to her.

Pauline admits that: 'It's hard to accept developing sexuality in your normal children; harder still in one with a mental handicap. If you admit it you may be expected to do something about it.'

She believes that a couple who have formed a close, loving relationship 'should be given guidance towards having a full sexual relationship by appropriately-trained staff. There are excellent training courses for staff who work with people with a mental handicap and there should be somebody locally they can be referred to. Parents certainly shouldn't be embarrassed about asking.'

She practises what she preaches. When her own daughter has had boyfriends, Pauline gave them every opportunity to be alone:

Unfortunately Diana, like many people with mental handicap, never achieved a full sexual relationship and that's sad. But the few relationships she has had went some way towards satisfying her emotional needs. And often it's simpler for parents than this. It may be just a case of letting someone know it's okay to touch themselves as long as it's done in private. Parents have to be understanding. You don't have to be an expert, just a human being who has had feelings of your own.

Of course, relationships are about a lot more than sex, and the more able people who can live together or get married must be taught about dignity and hygiene and looking their best, and that a woman's body is her own and she cannot be forced into sex.

One of the parents who admitted to a great deal of anxiety in this area of her daughter's life is Marion, whose 21-year-old daughter, Clare, has just returned home from 2 years away at a residential college. Clare, who has Down's Syndrome, is relatively able, though Marion doesn't anticipate her getting a paid job. She hopes she will be able to do some voluntary work. Marion:

Clare knows exactly what she wants. She wants to get married, as her sisters have. She has a boyfriend, John, who also has Down's Syndrome. We've striven to bring her up as normally as possible but honestly, the very idea of Clare and John setting up home seems ridiculous.

I've found it very hard to come to terms with this sexual aspect. Claire certainly likes boys. Before she went to college, she would get crushes on them, often boys we saw at church, and of course, she's not at all inhibited about letting on. She would go up and put her arms around them.

It was extremely embarrassing, but the boys coped very well and were always friendly and kind to her. Fortunately, we live in a village where everyone knows and accepts Clare. I think her interest in boys came as such a shock because, although her sisters had been through the same phase, they were obviously more controlled and discreet. With them it happened gradually; with Claire it seemed to happen overnight.

She's stopped running up to every boy she takes a fancy to now. Either she's passed through that stage or she's learned at college what's acceptable behaviour. Not that college, initially anyway, inhibited her. In fact it caused us more worry. She found a boyfriend, a very able, normal-looking lad, who really wasn't suitable for her. When we went to visit, she didn't want to know us. She kept running off with him, just to defy us, like a naughty teenager.

She told us she used to go to the woods with him and I'd be thinking 'What are they doing in the woods?', and hoping the staff kept an eye on them. We went to a few dances at the college and students would be kissing and cuddling on the dance floor, and the staff didn't seem to object. You don't want to seem a fusspot, forever asking questions. The whole idea is that they are young people now, not children, and should be given independence.

I must admit it was a relief when the first boy was replaced by John. He's more like Clare. We know his parents and they assure us he is not likely to have a full sexual relationship with a girl, although he is very physically affectionate with her. You try to be sensible and modern, but you do worry, don't you?'

SPEAKING FOR THEMSELVES

JENNY

Jenny has Down's Syndrome and has been having fits for the past five years. She lives in a suburban semi with her parents, June and Ron, and her 20-year-old brother, John. Jenny is 23.

June: 'In her body she's 23, but she's 6 years old in her mind. I've always said that and that's the way I treat her. I don't hold with pushing them out into the community and all this 'age-appropriate' stuff.

'She's not a 23-year-old woman in real sense. She needs supervising in everything she does. She's very lovable and she tries to do things for herself but she has no road sense, no sense of danger at all. If a perfect stranger knocked on the door, she'd open it and invite them in. And she needs her confidence boosting constantly or she won't do anything. You have to encourage her and tell her what to do several times and very simply.

'It's a cheek for a professionals to tell you what your child is capable of. The very most they could see her – and tell this is only a teacher or day centre staff – is around 25 hours a week. You, the parents, have her the rest of the time, 365 days a year. You know her. If Jenny goes away from home to live – and it would only happen if I was on my last legs – there's no way I want her forced into some kind of dodgy independence. I want her to be in a place, an ordinary house if possible, with trained staff living in to take care of her. What I want more than anything for Jenny is that she's safe.

'We've always taken Jenny with us wherever we go, but lately with the fits and everything I've been feeling worn out and we've started letting her go away for occasional weekends. When I first asked for respite care we were referred to a hostel, a great big place with rows of chairs in front of the telly and no waking nightstaff – horrible. I turned it down, then we went to see another place. This is a big old house, the staff are marvellous and they have a sort of baby alarm system so they can hear her at night. She goes for a weekend every eight weeks. I don't look forward to it, in fact I dread that weekend approaching, but once she's settled and I get away, I start to enjoy myself.'

June is a nurse and she had no doubt when Jenny was born that there was something wrong with her – she just wasn't sure what.

June: 'They'd taken my glasses away and I couldn't see her very clearly. By the time I got the glasses back they had taken the baby away to the nursery and the nurses made all sorts of excuses not to bring her back.

'They told Ron when he came in and he tried to tell me but he couldn't get the words out. He was mumbling something and I just said, "It's okay, I know."

'I was in a single room and the staff were very wary of leaving the baby with me. Apparently a mother had tried to harm a handicapped baby not long before, but I worshipped Jenny right from the start. There was never any question of me rejecting her.

'At one point the matron said to me, "Don't expect to take your daughter home." There are all sorts of questions you should ask when someone says something like that, but I never asked them. I just stared at her, confused. Obviously she was hinting that Jenny might not survive and I began to worry that they might think it would be better if she didn't, and not try too hard to feed her.

'After that I started going down to the nursery at feeding times and asking to give her the bottle myself, or watching the nurse while she did it. She was difficult to feed and when she'd stop sucking the nurses were inclined to stop trying, but I'd be there saying, "Go on, try again, she'll have it."

'I took her home at 9 days and for the first 3 years of her life she came to work with me. I was a trained nurse and the matron at my old hospital said they didn't want to lose me. She put me on a fairly easy ward, ambulant geriatrics. It was a very, very hard time for me but we needed the money. I was quite relieved when John came along because then there was no question of working.'

June says she has never left anything to chance where Jenny is concerned, but has pushed for her daughter's rights, starting with schooling.

June: 'At the time special schools weren't taking children with mental handicap until they were between 5 and 7 years old. If they didn't fancy them, they wouldn't accept them at any age. We decided to take matters into our own hands and looked up the addresses of all the special schools on this side of the city. We drove round to look at them, then rang the headmistress of the one we liked best and asked if she would see Jenny.

'She accepted Jenny to start at 4. I don't know why. Certainly it wasn't because she was not severely handicapped – she was one of the worst in the school. It was full mostly with what I call children with mild learning difficulties. There were always problems though. For a start they expected this 4-year-old with a mental age of 18 months to get there on public transport, three buses from where we then lived. There was a woman whose job it was to escort a group of them, but she'd have needed eyes in the back of her head and several sets of hands to do it properly. I banged tables, and shouted and stuck out for a taxi – and eventually we got one, all to herself. She rode up front with the driver.

'A little later we moved closer to the school and I started taking her myself. It was very important to me that I knew what happened, and the headmistress didn't exactly issue invitations, so I found an excuse to go in every day. There were lots of problems at the school. They started taking in very disturbed children and there were occasions when she was kicked and badly knocked about by these. I felt I had to find her a better place. She moved when she was 12, but at least that first school had taught her to read and write in a very simple way.'

June showed me examples of Jenny's childish drawing and writing, some of it just words jumbled up, others quite clear lines and passages copied from books. Among the drawings was written 'Romantic Lover Alan'.

June: 'She's made up this boyfriend; she call him Alan and says she's going to marry him. She likes boys – I suppose this is the one way in which she is older than a small child – but it's on a very superficial level. She likes to see people kissing on television: she thinks it's lovely. But this doesn't stretch to real life boys.

'I'd be worried if I thought there was a real boy in the picture, but I suppose if there was some sort of long-term relationship, I wouldn't object. At least I'd try not to. I would certainly have her sterilized in those circumstances. It's a small operation, with no side-effects and I can't understand why there's this agonizing over whether it's the right thing. It's just common sense.

'Sometimes if she's unhappy, you'll find notes around saying "I upset, I cry", which is just the way she talks. Her ambition is to be a secretary. They are planning to let her have some work experience at the centre, spending a few days in the office. It's a lovely treat, but nothing could come of it. I don't believe she could ever work, not even at the simplest job like tidying a room and washing up. She can do it, but she needs someone leaning over her shoulder telling her what to do, step by step. And then there are her fits, which prevent her doing a lot of things.'

Jenny's first fit occurred 5 years ago, at 4 a.m., while the family were on holiday.

June: 'We were staying in a chalet and the toilet block was about 50 yards away. Jenny woke and said she wanted to go to the toilet. We were half way there in pitch darkness, when she had a grand mal fit, complete with double incontinence. It was a nightmare. I couldn't carry her, so I had to virtually drag her back to the chalet.

'The fits have caused more stress than her mental handicap. You never know how bad they are going to be and she can have a dozen in quick succession. They often happen at night, so I feel safer if she's sleeping in my bed, but that causes problems with Ron. He thinks I'm babying her and he feels pushed out. I think men often resent the attention you have to give to a handicapped child – they want the attention for themselves.'

She thinks this feeling of 'not getting his fair share of attention' may have had something to do with the affair her husband had which almost broke up the marriage.

June: 'But I don't know. You can never be sure what starts these things. We're together still only because I hung on through all the humiliation. The best to come out of that awful time is that Ron now involves himself more with Jenny. For most of her life I felt I was looking after her on my own.'

Jenny was still at school, the one June had sought a transfer to, when her fits began.

June: 'It was a larger school with a high staff ratio including nursing staff, and she had the best days of her life there. I once asked her if she could have a wish what would it be and she said, "To go back to my school". She stayed there till she was 20 because Social Services hadn't provided places for school leavers in day centres. We parents made a lot of fuss, and in fact it was my suggestion to a councillor that got them to reopen the first school Jenny had attended and turn it into a day centre for adults.

'She goes there 5 days a week now and I can't say I'm happy with the place. They filled it up with hospital residents, who had a perfectly good centre of their own in the hospital, but there's all this business about getting them out into the community. There are frequent "exclusions", when they tell you to keep your child at home for days or weeks because of staff shortages.

'You never know what's going on. There's a lot of talk about things that are going to happen but they rarely materialize. If they do organize something it stops as soon as the kids get interested in it. Jenny went tap-dancing for 4 sessions and loved it, but when I asked if there would be a follow-up, they'd stopped it and moved on to something else. They say there is a timetable but that it's very flexible and can be changed at a moment's notice. I once took her in, all dressed up, for a Christmas party – only to learn it had been cancelled. She was so disappointed.'

June is adamant that as a parent you have to fight for every bit of 'welfare help' you get. She points out the brightly decorated little room dividing their living room from the back garden.

June: 'It took two years of fighting to get that built. We initially asked for a downstairs toilet because of the difficulty of getting her upstairs when she's having a fit. We were told that the local authority only has an obligation to provide downstairs bathrooms for people with physical disability, but we brought in a solicitor and challenged this. Eventually we got a shower room and toilet, but because of building regulations and the shape of the house it was necessary to cover in the area just outside the back door. So it was made into a little room and we furnished and decorated it for her twenty-first birthday. It's Jenny's little bit of independence, her study, and she loves it.'

ROBERT

Until 3 years ago, Robert was, in his mother's words, 'lovely, no trouble at all. You hardly knew you'd got him.' Then, without warning, at the age of 30, Robert's behaviour changed for the worse, putting enormous strain on his parents and on their 38-year marriage. The family live in a pleasant suburb. Robert's father, Bernard, is a medical technician. Robert was Stella's second child. There is a younger, adopted brother, now living away from home and a younger sister still at home. Robert attends a day centre and his mother, Stella, has enlisted the help of every respite service available to give the family frequent breaks.

They use a hospital repite care unit, a sitting service, and Stella gets a grant from the Independent Living Foundation, which pays for Robert to stay at the home of a carer for one or two weekends a month. This is a private arrangement between the two families, not a local authority scheme. Robert also goes to a weekly special night-school class and a club run by the nearby university. He spends alternative Saturdays at a 'play centre' run by a voluntary group.

Stella: 'You wouldn't believe it — 3 years ago, he'd never been anywhere. I had no contact with the welfare services or with anyone apart from the staff at the day centre. I looked after him myself, with a lot of help from his father. Now Robert's life has changed completely and so has ours.

'The crux of the problem is that he's developed this peculiar bit of behaviour right out of the blue. He just started turning round in circles. banging his left foot on the ground, moaning loudly and pulling his hair out. It sounds ridiculous put like that and not really anything to get het up about, but when it goes on and on, day after day, it just wears you down. There's no way to stop him, and being a big lad, over 6 feet, everything in the room shakes when he starts banging his foot.

'My husband was next door one evening when Robert was up to his tricks and everything in their living room shook too. The vibrations from the banging has been a little better since the local authority provided us with a special carpet and very thick underlay. It was a humiliating experience asking for this floor covering. They made us feel as if we were after something for nothing. I still have to cover the spot where he goes round with a spare bit of carpet or he'll wear a hole. There's not much you can do about the moaning. My daughter says she can hear him when she turns into this road on her way home from work.

'The mental handicap community nurses have been the greatest source of help and support. I didn't even know they existed before — my doctor had never thought to tell me. Technically I have a social worker. I know his name but I can't remember when I last saw him, and I didn't feel like asking him for help. It was a medical friend who put us in touch with the community nurses and other useful agencies.

'The community nurses call in regularly and they don't just talk, they get things done. One of Robert's other tricks was to bounce on the toilet till he's loosened the whole fitment. I asked social services for a frame to go around the toilet and I was told that there was a waiting list and I would have to wait till the occupational therapist could visit and assess the situation. I mentioned this to the community nurse we had at the time and she arrived a few days later with a frame in her car and set it up. Nine months later, I had a letter from the occupational therapist wanting to make an appointment to come and do the assessment!

'The only problem with the community nurses is that they keep changing. One will leave to have a baby, another to do a course, and they never seem to come back to your case. The present one, a man, is particularly good because he can talk to Bernard and Bernard tells him how he feels. I sometimes feel he's treating Bernard's problems as well as Robert's.'

Stella says that her husband has changed almost as much as her son over the past 3 years. On the face of it, this is a direct result of Robert's new behaviour pattern, but there was another change around the same time. As committed Catholics, the couple used to organize regular services in their parish church for people with disabilities. This had been a popular event for fifteen years when they were told that there were no longer enough priests to cope with all the weekend events at the church, and that theirs would have to be cancelled.

Stella: 'My husband went right down after that. He started saying that if even the church can't be bothered with people like Robert, why should we? He can't stand Robert around now. He goes mad when Robert starts his moaning. I believe he'd send him away tomorrow if we could find a place.

'It causes rows when I jump in to defend Robert. Often Bernard will go and sit in the other room, but you can't deaden the noise. I've tried everything I can think of to quieten Robert down. I've even tried smacking him but that doesn't work. Our doctor says we should put him in the back room, as far away as possible, and ignore him, but I couldn't do that.

'The only thing I can do to try and keep the peace is to get him out of the house as often as possible. If there's any function being put on by the mental handicap organizations, I make sure to take him. I don't know if the marriage can take much more. Sometimes I wish my husband would leave. It would relieve the tension, but I'm frightened of having to cope with Robert on my own. My daughter lives here, but she's rarely in – she has a life of her own. It's hard for her too, the bad feeling going on around her. She says she can understand how both of us feel, but she doesn't want to get involved. It's hard to believe that Bernard used to be so good with Robert, taking him out for walks and drives. Robert used to go everywhere with us. Despite his handicaps we were a very happy family.'

Stella: 'When I was in labour with my first child, there was a bright green show, which was an indication that the baby's heart was in distress. It was too late to do anything and she died. The doctor told me to carry on and have another; lightning doesn't strike twice, he said. But exactly the same thing happened with Robert and it took them 6 hours to organize a Caesarian. He survived but he was damaged. Nowadays you'd sue the hospital and have a good case.

'Robert fitted into the family well. I don't think the two younger ones ever suffered because of him. They were happy normal kids and brought their friends home. Robert loved having a lot of children around, the noisier the better. Nobody knows what caused this change in his behaviour. One doctor thought he might have had a slight stroke but there's no proof of that. I wonder if he hasn't just outgrown us and the house and become very, very bored in his own way. His brother has gone, his sister is not often here. It's become a quiet, dull place. He used to love to sit for hours in the front window, gazing out at the cars. But 33 years is a long time to spend watching cars go by. Maybe he's had enough.

'I know he's better when he's with a group of people and there's a lot going on around him. I took him on a holiday organized by a local group, just four of us mothers and our handicapped children. He was so good, almost his old self. Then, last summer, during his break from his day centre, I sent him to the local MENCAP summer play-scheme. They run one every year, for all ages, but I'd always kept him at home with me before and I felt quite guilty about sending him.

'One day they were short of volunteers and they asked me if I'd go in and help in the kitchen. It was a revelation. There was Robert, smiling, interested, watching the other people. There was no moaning and foot banging, he was no trouble to anyone. After that, I went in to help every day, though I hardly saw Robert. I was in the kitchen; he was out with the others having a good time.

I have asked about residential accommodation, but there's nothing suitable in the city, I'm told, and it might be five or ten years before a place comes up. Our local Social Services might pay for him to go to a home out of the city, but I don't want that. If he has to go away, I want him close by, where I can see him any time and he can come home to visit. But I'm in my late fifties now and I don't want to end up too old and ill to have any say in the matter. It's no good talking to my husband — he doesn't want any involvement. I just don't know where it will end.'

MICHAEL AND JULIE

Bob and Jean sit on either side of the fire, their grown-up son and daughter between them. It's a cosy family scene that's been repeated most nights for over twenty years. Michael and Julie (ages 30 and 26 respectively) are strapped into their wheelchairs. Michael looks around, Julie leans forward, her head hanging down. There is a towel in her lap. Occasionally her father wipes her chin with it in case she is dribbling.

Once Michael and Julie walked and talked, albeit belatedly, but gradually, over the years, their disabilities have become more severe. Soon these family nights around the fire and the television will be no more. In six months, they are leaving home to live in a purpose-built bungalow a few miles away.

Bob is an area manager for a chain of butchers. Jean says he could have been in a higher position by now or started his own business if they hadn't had to stay in the same place for the children. Bob says he probably wouldn't have; he's always been a stick in the mud! They lead a surprisingly normal life, which Bob puts down to Jean's organizational skills.

Jean: 'People ask how you manage with two, but they're not difficult kids. I know a family with a son who is much more able but he talks all the time, on and on, all day. Now that would drive me mad. Michael and Julie are easy people to be with. They have no illnesses – the only semi-medical thing I have to do is give them suppositories, and muscle relaxants for Michael. They are incontinent, but we get disposable pads delivered and picked up. We get a lot of help.'

Jean's day begins at 6.15 a.m.

Jean: 'At about 6.45 a.m, I wake the kids up gently, get them out of bed and feed them their cereal. Both have to be fed, but only Julie needs everything mushed. She fell and damaged her teeth, and though they're fine now, she got lazy and won't eat solids. At 7.30 a.m, the "bath lady" arrives. She's a nursing auxiliary who helps me bath them and get them ready for the day centre minibus which comes at 8.15 a.m.

'Then usually, they are out of the house till 4 p.m. When they get home, I toilet them and they have a cup of tea. When Bob comes home we all have our tea together. We feed them at the table as we are eating our own. We've always made a point of not excluding them. Afterwards they sit with us till bedtime at 9 or 10 p.m. If Bob and I are both home, we take one each and get them ready for bed. If one's out the other has to manage, but if we go out together, two sitters come in and carry out the same routine.'

As well as the sitters, they get a home help once a week and their children go for one weekend in six, plus a summer holiday, to a local short-stay home. This they pay for themselves, at a subsidized member's rate. The double mobility allowance has been used to buy a converted Nissan Prairie car, which has space for two wheelchair passengers in the back.

Their 3-bedroomed semi has been converted by the local authority; the dining-room turned into a downstairs bedroom and a bathroom built on.

Jean: 'Social Services didn't want to do it this way at first; they said it was too expensive. They wanted to put in a lift from the living room to one of the upstairs rooms. When I said we just hadn't got the space, a social worker told me, "You could get rid of some furniture; you've got far too much." But we stuck out for what we wanted.'

Michael and Julie were not obviously handicapped as babies or small children. Jean says they began to deteriorate around the age of 4, but claims not to remember much about those early days.

Jean: 'Maybe I've blanked it out. What I do remember, with Michael, are those awful visits to the specialist, this god, who looked at him briefly and said, "He's spastic, come back in six months." The whole attitude was, "Hurry up, the doctor's busy." When I did meet a doctor who treated me as an intelligent being and told me I knew more about my child than he did, it was marvellous. I remember there were a lot of tests, which kept proving negative. By that time we had Julie too, and they said it was some sort of genetic thing so having other children was out of the question.'

Bob: 'With Julie we were quicker to recognize the little signs, like the way she'd suddenly lose her balance when she was sitting. We were looking for it, you see. We had no idea that they would ever be as bad as this but there wasn't a sudden moment of realization because they've gone down hill so gradually. You just think one day, "Hey, Michael used to play with Lego, when did he stop?"

'I look at photographs and can hardly believe they're the same children. We've one of Julie standing up, laughing and waving streamers. You think, 'Was she ever really like that?' The one thing I was intensely aware of and found very upsetting was when Michael stopped walking and needed a wheelchair.

'The wheelchair, carried a lot of significance. It was a turning point that forced us to think about how he might end up. At first he pushed himself around in the wheelchair, but gradually that stopped. One day he just didn't do it any more and we had to accept that he never would again.'

Jean: 'The last bit of speech Julie hung on to was "Morning Mum". I'd say "Good morning" to her when I went in to get her up and she'd always answer. As time went on, I'd have to say it a few times before I got a reply, then one day I suddenly realized she hadn't said it for ages. And she never did again.

'We don't know if the deterioration has levelled out now. They certainly won't get any better. You always hope for a miracle. You hear of some new treatment and just for a moment you think, "Maybe..." though you know it's nonsense. I don't think either of us have felt bitterness though – it's nobody's fault.

'The hardest time for me was not when they were children, but now that my nieces and nephews have grown up and are having children of their own. I've found myself thinking, "We'll never have grandchildren," but I tell myself that neither will lots of other people, and those who have them often don't see them.

'Some of Bob's family have cut themselves off from us, but friends and family who have stayed around accept the kids completely. They are not handicapped people to them; they're just Michael and Julie who happen to be like this. They are very much individuals with different personalities. Michael is more "with it" than Julie. He knows what's going on and what you're saying. Julie always reminds me of Bob's mum – content to sit in a corner and watch the world go by.'

Given the circumstances, Bob and Jean have a good social life, each going out separately two nights a week while the other looks after Michael and Julie.

Jean: 'I had to nag Bob to find a hobby. Now he sings with a male voice choir and it's opened up a whole new social scene to us. I think it's vital to have outside interests. We get on very well but if we were sitting in every night we might get on each other's nerves.'

Bob: 'It also means I get two nights a week off from putting the kids to bed. It's not a massive job, but it hangs over you. You can't relax till it's done. When they are away for a weekend, I really look forward to putting my feet up and knowing I don't have to move again till I choose.'

Jean: 'We can forget about the kids and enjoy ourselves when we're not with them. We'd probably not have survived so well if we couldn't do that. Holidays, for instance – we are just a couple away together, having a good time. We rarely tell people we meet about Michael and Julie.'

Bob: 'I don't often tell people anyway. It's not that I'm ashamed or embarrassed. It's more that you don't want them making allowances, thinking, "What a shame, poor man...."'

Their ability to adapt to living without the children will be put to the test when Michael and Julie move into residential care.

Jean: 'We've been thinking for a while along the lines of "What will happen to them after we're gone?" Then both Bob's brother and brother-in-law were killed in separate accidents. It jolted us into realizing how unexpectedly something can happen, and we just wanted to get them settled.'

Through the computer-based organization Caresearch (which matches up residential accommodation available with those who need it) they found a small home, run by a resident couple. It was just what they wanted, but it was 150 miles away. Before they made any decision, they were told of a local housing project, close enough for Julie and Michael to continue at their present day centre.

Bob: 'Considering what an amazing stroke of luck it was, it took us a long time to say yes. Unlike the other place, there would be no mum and dad figure here, but staff who worked shifts, and the other residents were mostly older than our two. But we made the sensible decision and accepted. At least we'll be able to see them as often as we like.'

Jean: 'I'll have a hard job not poking my nose in. I know the staff won't do things the way I've always done them. It's the little things that upset you. When they come back from a weekend away, I can see that

Michael's ears haven't been washed properly and it irritates me. And I'd hate to think of someone else's clothes being put on them in a hurry.

'The truth is I'm dreading the day they go, but I'm trying to be positive because when I talk about it and get upset, Michael gets upset too. I look at his face and it's cross and unhappy and confused, and I know he understands. So now I tell him he's grown up and it's time for him to move away from home like his cousins have.

'I don't know how I'll feel. I'm the one it will make the biggest difference to. Bob will still have his work. My friends say I'm so bossy I'll have to find something or someone to organize. The one thing I know I'm going to enjoy – and probably only the mother of a handicapped child would understand this – is staying late at the shops. After a quarter of a century of rushing home to be there for the minibus, the freedom to hang around till the shops shut and wander home when I feel like it will be incredible.'

CARL

Carl lives on a large council estate with his mother, Heather, and his 29-year-old sister, Jacqueline. He is 25 and hyperactive. His mother gauges his mental age as around 3 years old. Heather is a widow; her husband, a car mechanic with his own small business, died recently of a heart attack. They were about to buy their house, but plans have had to be shelved, as Heather now has to live on a widow's pension plus Carl's allowance.

Heather admits to being anxious and stressed and 'living on her nerves'. She begins by describing Carl in optimistic terms: 'He's full of life, always trying to help you do things, like mow the lawn or paint a room'; and deteriorates into the pessimistic: 'He never stops going. You can't relax for a minute. Sometimes I think I'll go round the bend.' These views are different sides of the same coin.

Heather: 'He tries to do things for himself. He'll put his clothes on – but they'll be inside out or back to front. He can go to the toilet now, but he needs help. At the day centre, they never bother to wipe him after he's been and he comes home with soiled underpants every day. I have to have two dozen pairs so we don't run out. And he has accidents occasionally, at night. I could put him in nappies but it took me ages to get him out of them. I was very ashamed about having a big lad wearing nappies. I'd rather have the mess and the hassle than that.

'He's up till 10.30 p.m every night and he's running around all the time and fiddling with the television unless you can find something else that might occupy him. He plays his records so loud it drives me and Jacqueline mad. Jigsaw puzzles are the one thing that keeps him quiet for a while. I buy him the puzzles for 2-3 year olds – he can manage those.

'When Keith, my husband, was alive, he insisted that Carl have all his puzzles and playthings in the other room, but I thought why should he be in there on his own – it wasn't fair. So now it's just us, I have all his stuff in the main living room here and he plays with it while I watch television. At least that's the idea, but he doesn't like me having the television on. I'll turn it on, he'll turn it off again – and so it goes on. You can shout at him till you're blue in the face but he takes no notice.

'I love my son. I love every hair on his head, but sometimes it seems as if the last fifteen years have been like hard labour. Even the basic everyday things are such an effort. I have to wash him, clean his teeth, bath him. He's very dark and has a strong beard, so I have to shave him every day, while he objects and struggles. He hates anything being done to him.

'Weekends are the worst. It's impossible to keep him entertained at home so Jacqueline and I have to take him out. Since we don't have a car, it's bus rides. We go for miles. It doesn't really matter where, as long as he's going somewhere and there are people around. He loves people. We go to parks and shopping malls and different towns in the area, and we usually have fish and chips for lunch. He loves eating too.

'There's no way I could take him on my own. It takes two to handle him – one to hang on while the other pays the bus fare, or he'll be off down the bus, sitting by some stranger and trying to talk to them. He won't do them any harm, but people look a bit shocked.

'I daren't let him out of the house because he'll wander off out of the immediate area to a place where people don't know him. He can be very worrying for strangers. What would be perfect for Carl is a really big house where he could have an enormous sound-proofed room of his own, and he could do anything he liked in it. He could play music at full blast, splash paint all over the walls and run from one end to the other. This is such a little house. He's so cooped up in these rooms, it's like a prison to him.

'One place he gets a bit of space and freedom is at his clubs. There's one he goes to every fortnight at the MENCAP place. They have dancing there and he dances around by himself in a dream. He doesn't need a partner. There's another held monthly, and once a week he goes to a school where they have sort of night classes for handicapped people. They do hygiene with Carl, trying to teach him to clean, and they take him to the shops. They come and collect him in a minibus – he's out of the house about 3 hours.

'It's a breather for me, a few hours when I don't have to be thinking what to do with him next or trying to stop him doing something awful. And he loves to go out. Every night he asks "Club tonight?"

Every 5 weeks, Carl goes for a weekend to a Social Services hostel. He also spends a week there in the summer, so his mother can have a holiday.

Heather: 'He doesn't really want to go. He knows when he's going because he sees me packing his clothes, so that he can go there straight from the centre on the Friday afternoon. He watches me and he says, "Stay home". He loves his home and he loves me. I'm his whole life, really. When I've tried to go to night school, he's just cried all evening and Jacqueline can't handle him. Every night, in the early hours of the morning, he comes into my bed. He's always done it. When Keith was alive he'd snuggle down between us, now he gets into Keith's place. I'm with him too much, really.

'I send him away partly for my own sake, I admit it, but also partly because I think he should get used to being without me. I always tell him it's only for the weekend – even when he's going for a week. Well, he doesn't understand time. I'm always glad to see him when he comes back, but after a couple of days he's driving me round the bend again. He seems okay at the hostel but I don't go in or get too involved, because I'm afraid there might be something I don't like and then I wouldn't be able to let him go.'

Heather talks openly and anxiously about her finances.

Heather: 'I live on the £78 a week Carl gets – that's Invalidity and Attendance Allowances – plus £30 widow's pension. A night at the hostel costs over £5 and we spend a lot travelling round on buses. My husband worked very hard but he never made a lot of money. He worked for himself and there was no company pension plan or insurance. Sometimes I feel angry about that. I feel he didn't look to the future at all; he never considered what would happen to us if he wasn't here.

'I used to work when Carl was at a different centre, but the one he's at now, you have no idea what time the bus will turn up in the morning. It can be any time between 9 and 11, which means you can't keep to working hours. I don't even get Invalid Care Allowance – that stops when you get a widow's pension. The way things are now, I couldn't afford to let Carl live away from home permanently because I rely on his allowances to live.

'Carl never grieved for his father. Keith didn't spend all that much time with him – he was always out, either at work or fishing. I think it was Carl that drove him out in a way. He found the stress of him very hard to take. It did cause resentment. I used to think, "It's alright for him, he can walk out and get away from it." It's far easier to work – any sort of work – than look after someone like Carl. When his Dad died, I told Carl he'd gone to heaven. Sometimes now he'll look up and say, "Dad in the sky" but he also says "Dad gone out" and "Dad coming home." You don't know what goes through his mind.'

Heather describes her daughter, Jaqueline (interviewed on p.165), as 'golden', and says she couldn't manage without her.

Heather: 'She's been looking after Carl since she was just a child. Sometimes he gets on her nerves, of course, and sometimes the stress makes me and her get on each other's nerves. It's altered her life, definitely. She's never brought many friends home. It's not that she's ashamed of Carl, I'm sure, but this behaviour is a bit hard for outsiders to accept. You have to be very sure of people before you confront them with Carl.'

GETTING HELP

SPOD

Sexual and Personal Relationships for People with a Disability – includes mental handicap. They produce leaflets and books, run seminars and workshops and have a counselling line.

286 Camden Road,
London N7 0BJ.
Tel: 071 607 8851.

Friendship Schemes
Aim to link a person with a mental handicap on a one-to-one basis
with a volunteer, to share leisure time. There are several successful
projects up and down the country. Contact your Social Services
department or Citizen's Advice Bureau, or:

One-to-One,
404 Camden Road,
London N7 08J.
Tel: 071 700 5574 .
The latter has a list of schemes and can supply information on
setting one up.

4 The Special Problems of Older Parents

As parents grow older a subtle shift takes place. Gradually it becomes harder to be sure who is depending on whom. Is the parent looking after the son or daughter with mental handicap – or is it the other way round? Because those people still living at home when their parents are pensioners tend to be at the more able end of the spectrum, it's not as ridiculous a question as it might seem. Often there develops a mutually dependent relationship, emotionally and practically.

A mother in her late sixties, talking about her middle-aged daughter:

> If anybody had told me ten years ago that I'd be depending on Daphne to look after me, I'd have laughed, or maybe cried! But every stray bug lays me low lately and some weekends I'm fit for nothing except lying on the settee. She makes me sandwiches, and though I worry about letting her near boiling water, she makes me a lovely cup of tea. She's been a real little nurse. I couldn't manage without her.

And, of course, Daphne is dependent on her mother too.

Nor is it just a practical, physical dependency. Many parents, particularly the elderly widows, who are so often the only remaining carer, become emotionally dependent on their grown up 'child'. In a relationship of thirty or forty years' standing how could it be otherwise?

This is 78-year-old widow, Olive, talking about the reason she won't ask for a residential place for her 37-year-old daughter, Vicky.

> A good community nurse I had for a while introduced us to the home Vicky stays in. It's run by a voluntary organization and they charge nearly £200 a week, which I have been paying myself, though the Social Services department is going to help now. Vicky's very adaptable and she loves the home; she goes occasionally for

weekends, and for a month in summer while I visit my son in Canada. They've told me they'll consider her for a full-time place if I apply, but I'm afraid to ask in case they offer me one right away. I'm not ready to let her go yet. I live alone and the house would be so empty without her. I just couldn't bear to part with her, not while I know I'm able to look after her. I'd miss her so much.

And Gwen (75) talking about her hyperactive 40-year-old only child, Margaret, says:

A couple of vacancies have occurred locally over recent years that people told me would suit Margaret, but I've held back. I can't see her settling while my husband and I are alive. And to be honest, I can't see myself settling to living without her. She's such a big part of my life, I can't let her go. I'm selfish really.

The bond made up of love, duty and familiarity, and strengthened over decades, is hard to break. Sometimes, for an outsider, it's also hard to understand. The carer seems to have locked herself into a prison with only one other impossible inmate and thrown away the key. In other cases it's easy to see why they won't let go. As Harry, in his seventies, said about his 40-year-old son with Down's Syndrome: 'Life wouldn't be much fun without him. He's into pop music and all the latest crazes. He has us in stitches. It's like having a perpetual teenager in the house, but without the bad moods. He keeps us young.'

A mother in her eightieth year summed up a lot of older parents' feelings when she said of her 45-year-old daughter:

When she was born, when they told me she was handicapped, I thought it was the end of my life. Now I know she's the best thing that ever happened to me. Your other children drift away, but I've always been the most important person in Linda's life. Knowing she's there and needs me is what's kept me going all these years.

'A CONSTANT NIGGLING WORRY'

But, sadly, love isn't all you need. There's another side to caring into old age. The fear of being taken ill suddenly, of not being able to cope, is, as one mother put it; 'A constant, niggling worry that's with me when I wake up in the morning, and still there when I go to sleep every night.'

It's particularly worrying if you live alone. Lilian, first divorced and now widowed, and with no surviving children apart from 48-year-old Yvonne, is in this position: 'I dare not be ill. I will myself to stay healthy,' she says. No arrangements have been made for Yvonne should Lilian's willpower let her down. When she had to go into hospital for a hysterectomy recently, two friends, also mothers of daughters with mental handicap, each took Yvonne into their homes for half of Lilian's stay. One of the friends is older than Lilian.

Because she hasn't much confidence in Yvonne 'doing the sensible thing' in an emergency, like using the telephone or going to a neighbour for help, Lilian has arranged a signal with her neighbours. If her curtains are drawn back in the morning they know she is okay. If not, they are alerted to a possible emergency, which, fortunately, hasn't happened so far. The neighbours rise early, which cuts out any late leisurely mornings for Lilian, but she thinks it a small price to pay for peace of mind.

Sixty-eight-year-old Dorothy, crippled herself with arthritis, and looking after a very difficult daughter, wears a medical alarm pendant round her neck all the time. If she falls down and is unable to reach a telephone, she presses it and one of two named people is alerted to her predicament.

For some parents of sons and daughters who have an additional physical handicap, there is no question of going on caring indefinitely. They simply aren't physically able. One couple were managing to care for their son, who needs a wheelchair and weighs 12 stone, but talked of 'surviving on borrowed time'. May, the mother, explained:

> I have back problems from lifting. It's only because I get an allowance from the Independent Living Fund to pay for someone to help me in the morning that I manage. My son won't let us put him in a hoist – I think it frightens him. My husband helps when he gets home in the evening. I'm just hanging on till he retires in two years time, then hopefully, he can do the heavy lifting. You have to pray that his back doesn't go too. It's terrifying. You feel as if you're living on a knife edge, coping one day at a time, but I'd do anything to keep my son at home.

AFTER I'M GONE

It isn't only illness that preys on the mind. Parents of children with any serious disability think far more about their own death and its consequences than most people. The painful question, 'What will happen after I'm gone?' embeds itself in your consciousness at the earliest opportunity. With a bit of positive thinking and a lot of determination, it can be shoved to the back of the mind for years, erupting only at low moments and in the dead of a sleepless night. By the time you are drawing your pension, though, there's no way to avoid the question. It is suddenly in need of an urgent answer.

The single most important thing parents can do at this stage, if they haven't done so already, is to make a will. If somebody dies without doing so the beneficiaries are invariably left with problems to sort out. Should one of those beneficiaries have what the law describes as a 'mental disorder', the problems can be horrendous, with much of the legacy being eaten up in trying to sort out the tangled legal affairs.

You cannot leave a large sum of money or property to a person with a severe mental handicap, which renders him or her unable to handle their own affairs, so it is necessary to find a trustee or trustees and set up a trust. Often a trustee is a member of the family or a trusted friend; it may well be the same person chosen as executor of the will.

One major problem in leaving money for a person dependent on state benefits is that once the capital goes beyond a certain sum they will lose means-tested benefits like Income Support. The legacy will simply be used to replace it; in effect it will go to the state.

This can be avoided by setting up a carefully-worded discretionary trust. Making use of the various Income Support disregards, trustees can make small irregular payments to the beneficiary without affecting entitlement to Income Support allowance. The money can be used as the trustee and beneficiary see fit – for 'extras', like a holiday, a piece of expensive electrical hardware like a television set, or a special non-NHS wheelchair.

Some people choose to leave everything to their disabled child, often with agreement of their other children. Others, infuriated at the thought of losing their hard-earned and hard-saved money (some families save their child's welfare benefits in the belief it will buy a more secure future after they are gone) opt to leave everything to the able children and nothing to the one with a handicap, on the grounds he or she would never get it anyway. This doesn't necessarily work. The will may be successfully challenged by the local authority, which feels it has a right to a portion to help support the disabled person.

Some legal experts recommend a 50/50 split, or even leaving two-thirds for the normal children, one-third for the one with mental handicap. It depends a lot on individual family circumstances, and it is essential to have the will drawn up by an experienced solicitor. Staff at MENCAP's legal department are willing to speak to any solicitor involved in such a will. They also issue a leaflet *Leaving money by will to people with a mental handicap*. Gerald Sanctuary's book *After I'm Gone* (Human Horizons series, Souvenir Press Ltd) is a mine of rather complicated information. Unless you're a bit of an expert already, you do need someone, face to face, talking through the will-making process and explaining the small print.

The second most important thing to do – and most parents realize it – is to find a residential placement for their son or daughter while they are still reasonably fit and able to help them settle in. But hearts and heads don't necessarily agree and parents can't always bring themselves to do the right thing. Sometimes they can't let go because nothing that is available seems good enough. Sometimes it's because they know their son or daughter will be unhappy anywhere but home, and they cannot bear to see that unhappiness and be party to it. And, perhaps more often than is admitted, what stops them is the thought of their own loneliness and loss.

A couple of parents, quite rightly, scoffed at the apparent suggestion that there was a host of alternatives waiting for their child and they only had to ask to be offered a place. There is a dearth of residential places. The greater the handicap, it seems, the fewer the places available. Even the hospitals, which used to take the more severely handicapped, are being run down; many have already closed.

Professionals talk of an ideal of normalization, of community life in an ordinary house in an ordinary street. Parents long for sheltered, lifetime care in an environment that is, above all, safe. Home Farm Trust and the Care villages are mentioned often. Their nightmare is of their child sharing a scruffy house with others no more able than himself, unsupervised, unloved and exposed to danger in a community that avoids him. This, they say, is not progress, and they've seen it happen.

The ideal situation, many said, would be a local, staffed unit where their son or daughter could get used to short-term care, with the assurance that there would be a full-time place available when needed. Unfortunately, it doesn't happen very often; people have respite care in one place and will be whisked off to wherever there is a bed available when parents become ill or die. No unit can guarantee a vacancy to order.

Occasionally a brother or sister will offer to take the sibling with learning difficulties into their own home. Some parents hope this will happen, but most think it unlikely and many wouldn't accept the offer if it were made. Too risky, they said; what if the arrangement broke down? Then there would be an extra trauma for their child to face. And in any case, they wouldn't want another, equally loved, child to suffer the responsibilities and privations they have lived with.

BEREAVEMENT

It doesn't take much imagination to guess at the shattering effect on someone with a mental handicap, who has lived at home all their life, of losing a parent, particularly the one remaining parent. Quite apart from the practical issues of who will look after them, there is the pain of loss and, in some cases, an inability to understand what has happened. One of the mothers, near to tears, explained: 'I can't bear to think of him waiting and searching for me, not knowing why I've left him.'

It wasn't necessarily the people who appeared most able who grieved most. Vicky is relatively able but, according to Olive, her mother, didn't exhibit any distress when her father died.

You see, I don't think she knows he's gone for good. It's still as if she's waiting for him to come back, despite the years that have passed. Sometimes she will say, 'Daddy is with nurse Abigail.' That was the name of one of the nurses who was with him when he was last in hospital. She has never cried about it, though she loved him dearly. I just pray she takes my death the same way.

Yet Susan, who seems much more handicapped, still weeps uncontrollably when she sees a photograph of her father, two years after his death.

It's generally accepted that most bereaved people with mental handicap grieve just as the rest of us do, though it can't always be conventionally expressed, and sometimes comes out in disruptive behaviour or regression. It's also noted that the grief reaction may be delayed. It almost goes without saying that they should be offered comfort and specialized counselling and encouraged to talk, if they can, about their feelings and about the dead parent. But sometimes, in the confusion that can follow a death, busy staff may not have the time, the experience or the knowledge to even notice the distress. One of the worst things that can happen is a 'conspiracy of silence', where everyone avoids talking about the parent, for fear of upsetting the bereaved person. The well-meant dishonesty leaves them more confused and unable to accept what has happened.

Maureen Oswin, who has written a book on the subject, feels strongly that there must always be honesty, with the bereaved person being kept informed of what is happening, taken to the funeral and given extra contact, understanding and support for as long as the grieving lasts – and that can be years. Even those who cannot understand the concept of death – and many of the parents I talked to were unsure if their son or daughter could – will feel the acute pain of separation and loss.

Maureen Oswin also suggests that, where possible, someone with severe handicaps should not be whisked away from their home as soon as the parent dies. Ideally, they should stay in the home for weeks or months with someone moving in to care for them, while learning to accept what has happened and being introduced gradually to a residential unit. It's a very painful problem and most parents push it aside in favour of the more practical, but still difficult, issues of where their child will live after their death.

Two simple but sensitive books for reading to, or with, someone of any age with mental handicap are *When Dad Died* and *When Mum Died*, by Sheila Hollins and Lester Sireling, published by Silent Books, Swavesey, Cambridge.

THEN . . . AND NOW

Inevitably there was a lot of looking back, and not always in anger. Lilian, whose second handicapped child had spent the last 4 years of his life in one of the now-reviled mental handicap hospitals, regretted its demise:

> They weren't all tarred with the same brush. My son's hospital was a good place. The staff were caring and the residents had all the facilities they needed on the site. They could have done up the hospitals and improved the staffing. Instead they discarded them and turned the residents out to live in boarding houses and group homes.

But the good days were not all good for Lilian: 'I don't know how I managed. I couldn't have without my parents after my marriage ended. I used to go to work, rush home to see my daughter, then off to the hospital to spend a couple of hours with my son and get him ready for bed. If I got ill and couldn't work there would be no money. There were none of the benefits you get today.'

Today's benefits are accepted gratefully, but not always understood. One woman explained: 'It's very confusing. I don't know what I can claim. They send forms to my daughter, demanding to know about her spouse and children. I tell them these questions are not relevant but they still keep asking.'

'I'm not one of those people who are all grab, grab, grab,' another said. 'Sometimes I'll bump into another mother and she'll say: "Have you applied for such-and-such an allowance?" I can't bring myself to keep applying, keep asking. It's too much like the begging bowl. My daughter and I can manage. It makes me mad though when I hear of others getting hundreds of pounds. The system isn't fair. It should be the same for all.'

The greatest dissatisfaction was with day centres. The dropping of contract work for students who could manage it and the change in emphasis to social and out-of-centre activities pleased no one in this age group.

Short-term care is also a prickly subject, to be approached sensitively with parents who have managed without it for thirty-odd years. Some of the more innovative ideas were met with total shock. Olive had suddenly found herself with a young social worker, having not seen anyone from his department for years. His enthusiastic explanation of a shared care scheme he was setting up, whereby a person with learning difficulties could have periods of respite care with a family who would be trained, paid and formally vetted, horrified her: 'Well, there would be a man in the family, the husband, and possibly grown-up sons too. They could take advantage of my daughter. I said certainly not.'

A more cynical assessment of the scheme's failing was given by another mother. 'Who would want to take a disagreeable, middle-aged woman with a mental handicap into their home? It'll never get off the ground.'

If anyone doubts that older parents are under stress, they should read a report by the Spastics Society, *Still Caring*, published in 1990. The researchers concluded that older parents are caught in a moral trap, obliged to look after their middle-aged 'children' even when they are unable to cope properly any longer. Over four-fifths of those interviewed had health problems, and over half were emotionally stressed. The report criticized the government's community care plans, due to start in 1993, for urging carers to carry on, without considering their right to stop.

But despite all their problems, these parents are made of stern stuff. Most of those I spoke to were determined to carry on caring, and in a letter to a newspaper just before Mothers' Day, the Smethwick Society for Mentally Handicapped Children and Adults, praised some of their women members. Thirty of these women had been caring for their son or daughter for over 30 years, 7 for over 40 years, 4 for 50-plus years. One indomitable lady in her ninety-first year was still looking after two disabled sons at home. 'The best mothers in the world', the writer said. And who could disagree?

SPEAKING FOR THEMSELVES

BRENDA

'Come on in love.' Brenda opened the door while her mother, Elsie, struggled to lock a noisy dog in the kitchen. She is 47, plump, matronly, sociable – a middle child, sandwiched between two brothers.

Her mother, Elsie, widowed 14 years, is now 78. They live together in a council house, which seems to be partly furnished by the end-products of Brenda's night-school classes in carpentry! She proudly points out a stool, a table and some shelves she made. She also made the skirt and blouse she is wearing – in her needlework class at her day centre.

'She does cookery at night school too, but what she turns out there isn't worth boasting about,' Elsie says. They tease each other companionably. Brenda says, with much giggling, that her mother was sent a bottle of whiskey by her boyfriend – an elderly pensioner from bingo, disowned by Elsie.

Brenda's handicap, Elsie says, is 'due to neglect'.

Elsie: 'I had bad toxaemia which wasn't treated and the poison from my kidneys went to her brain. They didn't think she'd live. Her weight went down to 2lbs 11oz. She was christened at 2 days old. Ages afterwards our doctor told me he thought I was nursing a dying baby, but he never said anything at the time because if she was to have a chance it was important I should breastfeed her. He didn't think I'd be able to if I thought she wasn't going to live.'

Even so, it wasn't until Brenda was 3 years old and not walking that the family doctor confirmed that she was 'backward'. Elsie says she was told there was an operation which might help, but that if it failed Brenda would be a 'vegetable'.

She doesn't know the nature of this operation and in any case, she declined. Brenda walked when she was 6, and started attending a special school for the mildly handicapped at 10 years old.

Elsie: 'When she didn't learn to read and write within a year, they said she couldn't go again. Well, it's daft. Lots of normal kids don't do all that in a year. I appealed and I had to take her to a horrible man. I don't know what his position was, but he did these silly tricks to assess her ability. We ended up having an argument. I called him a bloody fool and he threatened to take me to court, which was nonsense.

'They didn't have her back at the school and she started at a centre for the handicapped which was held in a church hall. That place had it's problems – the caretaker often left the heating off in the coldest months, and the kids had to be wrapped in blankets to try and keep warm. But they taught her useful things. One of the things she learned was which knives and forks to use at a meal. You could take Brenda to the poshest hotel in town and she wouldn't let you down. At first I used to have to take her to and from school myself, but then they got a guide who was paid to take three or four of them in on the bus together.

'There were no schools as such in those days for kids like Brenda. There was precious little help of any kind! No welfare benefits like today. When she was 16, she was awarded the princely sum of £1.50 per month. Today there's financial help from babyhood; too early if you ask me. They don't cost much more than any normal child at that age.'

Brenda moved from the junior centre to the adult centre at 16. She is still there, although the centre has changed its name and its philosophy, which dismays Elsie.

Elsie: 'The previous manager there, now he was a charming man. He understood the kids and the parents. Brenda used to do a little job – she packed plastic cutlery for airlines. She was paid £1.20 per month and when she got that money, her face would light up. Some of the students made things that could be sold at the Christmas fair towards a party or days out, which the kids loved.

'Then new people with new ideas came in to run the place. They got rid of the work, said it was cheap labour. Instead the kids watch videos, go out to the shops, maybe do a bit of sewing. They are bored to death and there's not one parent satisfied. They *need* something to do. They like to have a little job if they're able. It's not cheap labour, it's occupational therapy.'

If Brenda's days are boring, her nights certainly aren't. She goes to bingo in the church hall twice a week with her mother, and on regular church outings. There's carpentry and cookery, a MENCAP club twice each month, another once-a-week club for people with disabilities.

Elsie: 'They transport her in a social services minibus or cars driven by volunteers. Brenda loves it. At the clubs it's mostly dancing and meeting her friends. She has two boyfriends – a big smile and a nod of agreement from Brenda – but she only sees them there. It's just friendly, no hanky-panky.'

Elsie admits she would be shocked and angry if she ever found that Brenda was having a sexual relationship.

Elsie: 'It would be proof she hadn't been supervised or looked after by somebody, wouldn't it? She did once tell me she'd like to get married, but I said to her, "If you do that you won't be able to live with your Mom and you'll have to cook and clean for your husband every day." She decided that maybe she wouldn't after all!'

To be on the safe side though, Elsie had Brenda sterilized.

Elsie: 'You hear such a lot about girls being abused. She's very affectionate and friendly. It wouldn't be hard for someone to take advantage of her. And she certainly couldn't look after a child. The do-gooders who say girls like Brenda have the right to have babies simply don't know our kid. While I'm here I can protect her but will they be as careful of her in a home or a hostel?

'I asked our doctor about sterilization and he referred me to a specialist who wanted to know if Brenda understood what the operation means. I said I'd explained as best I could. He talked to her a little bit, then he said, "Brenda, you won't be able to have babies if you have this operation. Do you want babies?"

"Don't be stupid," she said, "I couldn't look after a baby." He went ahead with the operation.'

Elsie rubbed a painful, bandaged knee as she talked. She has arthritis and a heart problem and recently lost a stone in weight. She has not been well for some time, she says. However, until 7 months ago, she had no contact with any social worker, community nurse or other professional, apart from Brenda's centre.

Elsie: 'It had been years since I'd seen a social worker. I didn't even know where to find one if I needed to; they've moved since I was last in touch. We've not needed anything, Brenda and me, so I've never bothered with them.

'But lately I've been feeling bad. I couldn't even take Brenda to the dentist when she had toothache so I sent a note to the centre asking if someone there would take her. They must have got in touch with Social Services and a nice young chap came to see me.

'He not only took her to the dentist in his car, but he wanted to know if she'd ever been away to give me a break. I said no, and he started pressing, very gently like, for me and Brenda to go and see the hostel for our area.

'He drove us over. It seemed very nice, and while we were there, they asked Brenda if she'd like to come for tea on her own another day. She agreed and when she went to tea they asked her if she'd like to spend a weekend. And so on, always getting Brenda to agree. She's been for 3 weekends now and this month she went for 5 days. It costs £16 for a weekend and £37.50 for 5 days, which comes out of her allowance.

'When she's there they take her out to barbecues, to discos and to church. They never let them come home with dirty washing. They teach them how to wash and iron their own things. Brenda irons lovely now; she never could before. She's very happy at the hostel and it's a great load off my mind.

'She did say to me once, "You're not trying to get rid of me, are you?", and of course I'm not. She's good company for me. I miss her when she's away. But I'm so relieved she's got somewhere else to go if I get ill, or if I die.

'I've talked to her about this, about dying, and she accepts it, don't you, Brenda? (Brenda nods.)

'And they've talked to her at the hostel. She knows that she will live at home with me till I am no longer able to look after her or I pass away, and then she'll go to live there. They have promised me there will be a place for her.

'I don't want either of my boys to have her. Well, you can't lead a normal life. It upsets the older one, that she's got to go to a home, but I say, "What if you had her then found you couldn't cope? She'd have to go somewhere else and that would be a double trauma." That's my way of looking at it.

'She'll be all right at the hostel. I wouldn't want her living in a house with no staff though. She wouldn't starve – she can make a cup of tea and toast – but she can't cook properly. She's afraid of the gas. And she's got no road sense at all. The boys will keep in touch, and my brother and his wife and my nephew and his family will have her out to tea sometimes. Yes, I'm sure she'll be all right. And I couldn't have said that 6 months ago.'

SUSAN

For all but 5 days of her 39 years, Susan has lived at home with her parents, all day, every day. The 5 days away, when she was 15, were spent at a special hospital, an experience so horrific that her parents,

John and Dorothy, vowed never to let her out of their care again. Prior to this, she had been rejected by a special school because staff thought her too difficult to handle.

Susan is still difficult, though her mother insists she has improved a lot in the past 15 years. She has Down's Syndrome, but is much more handicapped than the average Down's person. Dorothy believes she was additionally damaged by a vaccine when she was young, but has not been able to get compensation for this.

She walks a little, but is so unpredictable – she may sit down in the middle of a busy road and refuse to budge – that she was awarded mobility allowance. Small and plump, she spends most of her time in one room, the family living room, throwing playing cards into the air. Along with brown paper bags, cards are her favourite playthings. She doesn't always welcome visitors and is not above giving them a sharp pinch or a kick in the shins if not restrained!

At night, Susan, who sleeps in a downstairs room with her mother, is restless and needs attention. Since John died, looking after her has been an exhausting 24-hour-a-day job for 68-year-old Dorothy, herself virtually crippled by osteoporosis. Another daughter, Jane, married but childless, is a doctor working in medical research and lives about a hundred miles away.

Dorothy: 'I remember saying to John, "If anything happened to you, I couldn't cope.", but you do somehow. You just get on with it. You can get used to anything. And he wasn't a father who said a few words to her when he got in from work and left all the work to me. From the time she was 5 he slept in her room so that he could see to her when she woke in the night. It was a kind of shift system. I did days, John did nights. After he retired he used to take her for a walk twice a day. She misses him dreadfully, though she can't tell you. Even now, if her attention is attracted to a photograph of her father, she'll pick it up and cry over it.'

Dorothy believes that Susan was born a 'high grade Down's child' and that that her brain was further damaged by a diphtheria injection when she was a toddler.

Dorothy: 'She was making good progress and starting to talk. After the injection it all stopped. We couldn't get any compensation as they said she was already mentally handicapped anyway, which is very unfair, because she could have been a far more able person.'

Initially the family wanted Susan to go to school, but when she was rejected they concentrated on bringing her up at home and never again sought a school or day care placement. Only dire necessity forced them to ask for a short-term residential place at a nearby mental handicap hospital, when Dorothy needed an operation.

Dorothy: 'Susan was 15, Jane was involved in her A-levels and John was working. I didn't like the idea of Susan going away, but it seemed the most sensible option. We took her down to the hospital on the Friday. Oh, my goodness, it looked awful! Inside there was this big hall, with music blasting out and benches all round the walls.

'They told us not to come again for a few days, to let her settle in, but John went on the Sunday. When he came back he was so upset. I'd never seen him cry, but he cried then. I knew I couldn't go into hospital the next day and leave her in that place so I asked him to go and fetch her.

'By the time he got back there, she was in bed. They had to get her up and dress her and he carried her all the way home. She was in a terrible state. You'd wonder how she could get that bad in 3 days. She was completely dehydrated – I don't believe a drop of water had passed her lips. Her lips were cut, there was a burn mark on her cheek and one eye was shut. She looked like something out of a horror film. We knew then we could never let her go away again, however great our need.

'But it isn't only for Susan's sake that I couldn't subject her to being in some unsuitable place. If something distresses her, I get the subsequent tantrums. She apparently blamed me for putting her in the hospital and for ten years I had to bear the brunt of this anger. The years between 15 and 25 were absolute hell for me. She wouldn't go into anyone else's house without one of us behind her pushing her and another in front pulling. She must have thought we were going to leave her again.

'At home you had to watch her every second of the day. She would pick up and throw anything she could put her hands on. The amount of crockery we got through! Finally, I went out and bought her an enamel cup, saucer and plate and do you know, she never threw that. She knew it wouldn't break.

'Sometime, around the age of 25, Susan changed. I've no idea why. From being doubly incontinent, she began using a potty – well, it's a bucket actually, that's what she prefers. She stopped throwing things, except for cards and bits of paper. Some day's she'll even watch a bit of television, and she tolerates outsiders much better. The only time I heard her speak a whole sentence clearly though was when she was around 20 and we'd dragged her into the house of a relative who had a baby. Sitting on the settee she suddenly announced, "Auntie's baby is happy." She said it twice, clear as a bell. That's the only time I ever heard her deliver a whole sentence in the correct place, though she does say certain phrases if you can understand her.'

As we talked Susan would come towards us saying what Dorothy translated as, 'Stop it, you two.' Dorothy would stand up painfully and lead or cajole her back to her chair.

Dorothy acknowledges that she would not be able to keep her daughter at home without a great deal of help. When her husband, a very independent man, was alive they accepted very little help. Now she uses a sitting service to provide two care assistants twice each day, paid for by the Independent Living Fund. The aim of the Fund, financed by the government and administered by the Rowntree Trust, is to keep disabled people in their own home, by providing the financial assistance to buy-in care. Usually the care assistants take Susan for a walk.

Dorothy: 'They can't go far because she won't walk long distances, but it gives her a change of scene and she enjoys it. Sometimes, instead, they come out in the car with me and Susan, and I sit in the car park while they fetch my shopping. I can walk as far as the car, and I can drive, but my condition makes it impossible for me to walk round the shops. It's very frustrating.'

Courtesy of the local authority, Dorothy also has a home-help one day each week, and a night-sitter to ensure she gets at least one night of unbroken sleep in a separate room.

Occasionally, she uses her Independent Living Fund cash more adventurously. With the help of a care assistant, she took Susan for a four-day holiday last year. It cost £240 to pay the sitter for day-work only, but she says it was worth it. She also saved up some of the money to help pay the £1,100 it costs to provide home-based care for her daughter, while she, Dorothy, was in hospital for an operation.

Dorothy is used to people trying to persuade her to send Susan to a day centre. They insist it would be good for both of them – Dorothy would gain some freedom and Susan would get a taste of the ouside world and a bit of variety in her life.

Not to be churlish, she says, she recently accepted the invitation of a social worker to visit the nearby adult training centre.

Dorothy: 'I was disgusted with the conditions. The place was smelly and, as far as I could see, there was only one person in charge of a room full of quite handicapped people. There is no way I would send my daughter there.'

Susan's future is a constant source of anxiety to her mother, but she worries a little less since she devised a plan which she hopes will ensure home-based care for the rest of her daughter's life. The plan, worked out with solicitors, is timed to come into effect on Dorothy's death. She has savings which will continue to bring in interest at the rate of £60 per week; Susan has mobility and disability benefits. If, in addition, she continues to get the Independent Living Allowance, there should be sufficient to pay someone to live in the family home to take care of Susan.

There is no question of Jane, the other daughter, who has a demanding career, taking Susan into her home, but she has agreed to oversee her mother's plan with the help of a solicitor. Will it work?

Dorothy: 'I hope so. I can't bear to think of Susan in some institution. She's lost her father, she'll lose me, but she shouldn't also have to lose her home and all the familiar things she has grown up with. I hope and pray it will work, but I'll never know. That's the awful thing. But at least I've done my best.'

BOB

Bob pokes his head round the door, a big grin on his face, and a sink plunger held to his forehead.

'I am a dalek . . . ex-ter-min-ate . . .'

'You can see why we like having him around,' his father says. Bob, who has Down's Syndrome, is 40 going on 15. He is polite, friendly and full of fun, though his parents, Harry and Peggy, both in their early seventies, say he has quietened down in recent years. The couple have one older son, Ian, who is married with a family. They live in a comfortable suburban home. Harry is a retired commercial artist. Peggy worked as a dinner lady. 'You're so tied to time with someone like Bob you can never hold down a good job.'

Bob attends a day centre, but otherwise spends little time apart from his parents. They take him to the theatre, on all sorts of outings, and abroad on holiday.

Harry: 'We're very lucky really. People like him. You can take him anywhere and he'll enjoy it. When we're on holiday and there's dancing or entertainment, he's the first one up there joining in, while we sit on the sidelines. I've never known him to be bad-tempered or bored, not for a minute. Some nights he'll be up in his room listening to records; other nights he'll be down here with us.

'We're very involved with the local MENCAP society and Bob goes to their evening clubs. I usually take him over. He has a great time. He's very popular with the opposite sex. Any night you're liable to find some girl crying because Bob isn't being friendly enough to her. He goes for huge girls twice his size, but there's nothing serious in it.

'Besides, he has his girlfriend. He's going to California to marry one of "Charlie's Angels", Jaclyn Smith. The series has been off television for years but he's faithful to her. He tells everyone. I don't know if he believes it or he's having us on. I tell him he can't go to California until he learns to read and write and he shrugs and says, "Okay".

'And that should be a long time. He can't read, write or count beyond ten or remember what day it is. Occasionally you'll get a new person at the centre who's convinced they can teach him, but they give up in the end.

'I don't know why he can't learn. He has no trouble picking up how to work his record player or the video recorder. I feel we missed the tide with him. He's on the downward swing now. If he'd been taken in hand when he was younger, the way Down's kids are today, a lot could have been down with him.'

Peggy and Harry were not told about Bob's condition at birth. They didn't know he was in any way different to their older son until he was 5 or 6 months old.

Peggy: 'We must have been very thick, but he developed fairly normally at first. I used to notice the nurses at the clinic looking at him strangely. Finally I asked on of them if there was something wrong and she said she'd like me to see a specialist.

But, even then, the specialist didn't tell me. All she said was that this baby was going to cause me a lot of trouble. I couldn't stand it any longer and stormed round to my GP and demanded to know what was wrong with my child. He told me that Bob was mentally retarded, and said he'd like to see Harry that evening to explain more.'

Harry: 'He explained it a bit more to me all right. He said the baby was a mongol and would never look after himself, but we weren't to worry because they never lived past 16. He seemed to think that was the good news. He also suggested we have another baby straight away and when I asked about the possibility of having another one the same he said it had never been known to happen. When I got involved with the local MENCAP society I found out that was a fairytale; there were several people with two in those days.

'I suppose you can't blame the doctor for his ignorance. It was the dark ages as far as mental handicap was concerned. We'd never seen another Down's kid. People kept them hidden.'

Peggy: 'We were both terribly upset. I pleaded with God to take him back. It was very hard facing people; there were some funny ideas around. I was sitting on a bus with him one day and a woman opposite said to her friend, "That's what happens if you try to get rid of a kid before it's born." I was so upset. Bob was very much a wanted baby. We'd been trying for him for 4 years. I think the turning point, the point at which I started really accepting him, came when I'd taken him into a cafeteria for a meal and a woman kept staring. I turned right round in my chair and stared back at her. She got flustered and embarrassed. I thought – why the hell should I care what other people think? He's my baby and I love him.'

Harry: 'He was a terror as a child, a real livewire. We used to spend most of our time on holiday chasing him around crowded beaches when he ran away. In the end we discovered the only way to get a few minutes peace was to tie him to the deckchair.'

Peggy: 'But the doctors were wrong. They told me he'd never be clean, and he was out of nappies by the age of 2. They said he'd never talk – he's hardly stopped to draw breath. He has a good vocabulary, but there's a slight speech defect which can make him hard to understand. He goes red with effort sometimes when you're not taking it in. He'll never be palmed off with you saying, "Oh, yes" and pretending you know what he's on about.'

Bob attends a local day centre.

Harry: 'They're just babyminders at the centre now. It used to be different when they gave them work to do. Now it's more or less what he had in the church hall he went to as a child. At one time wild horses wouldn't keep him away, but when he started back after the last break you'd think he was going to be shot.

'But he settles to most things. He can always find something he likes. One day each week the more able ones from the centre, Bob among them, take old ladies out shopping. He loves that. What he really enjoys though is simple repetitive work that would bore us to death. Ideally, I'd like to see him in a sheltered workshop.

'He treats us a bit like old folk now, taking our arms to see us safely across the road! It makes you laugh, but you do get situations where the handicapped child ends up looking after the parents. He's wonderful to us. He helps with the housework — poor little drudge! He washes the car and because I've got angina, he's the one who clears the snow away in winter.'

Peggy: 'We'd never leave him alone but Harry's sister lives with us and occasionally we go out without him. His last words to Harry are always: "Take care of my Mum." He gets very worried if we're a bit late.'

Talk of age and health leads on to the subject of mortality and Bob's future when his parents are no longer here. Peggy loses her cheerful bantering tone.

Peggy: 'I dread waking up in the night because it's always the first thing on my mind — what will happen to Bob? It goes round and round unanswered. We know Ian, our older son, would do his best but he has his family. We don't expect him to take Bob into his home. I suppose he'll have to go to a hostel, but who knows what is going to be available in a few years' time?'

Harry: 'Twenty years ago, when hostels were the great new thing, I thought that by the time Bob would need them they'd have been perfected; places of excellence. It hasn't happened. Now we hear they are much too large and institutional, and kids like Bob are being shoved into little houses to fend for themselves. They say it's the latest thinking. Who's doing this latest thinking? Usually someone six months out of college with no experience. They seem to think that if they pretend these kids are not handicapped they'll become normal. Whatever you do, they'll still be inadequate in many ways.

'The new thinkers talk about giving them freedom, but they are only giving them freedom to wander around the streets looking bedraggled and unkempt. It may look good on paper, but the reality is that these kids end up living in squalor.

'And the hostels are not much better. Depending on the whims of the staff they are either pushing them out every night to get 'A' levels or something, or they are like old people's homes. There's no happy medium. Our ideal is something like a Home Farm Trust, where residents live out their lives in the security of a nice safe environment, with work to do and people to care for them. The kids like it; the parents like it; what does it matter if the professionals don't like it?'

Peggy: 'Maybe if Bob could move into the same place as his best friend, Peter, it mightn't be too bad. We've thought about it – Peter's mother too – but we've never made a move. We keep leaving it and leaving it. Ian says we are being selfish because at this rate he's going to be the one to have to put Bob away after we're gone.

'We're leaving money in a trust fund for Bob, so he won't be poverty-stricken. But, basically, he doesn't need much money. It can't buy the things he needs. What I dread most is him being expected to manage on his own. He could cook an egg; he can make a damn good cup of tea; but he has a skin complaint that needs watching, he has ingrowing toenails. Who'll bother with these little things?'

Harry: 'There's just one possibility I'm pinning my hopes on. Did you know people with Down's Syndrome get Alzheimer's disease early? Of those who live to be 60, 96 per cent get it. I know because Bob is involved in a research project with a teaching hospital. Our families, on both sides, have lived into their nineties. At the back of our minds, we feel if we could hang on another twenty years, we might outlive Bob. He might never have to go away. It's a terrible thing to hope for but it's the best of the options.'

YVONNE

Yvonne is 48, and her mother Lilian's only surviving child. Lilian's only other child had multiple handicaps and died in his twenties. Her marriage broke up when the children were young and she brought them up alone with the help of her parents. Lilian is 75 and was a teacher in a school for children with mental handicap.

Lilian: 'I get very depressed sometimes. I look back and think – what a bloody awful life. It's lonely anyway being old, but when you have a handicapped child you are cut off. There's a great weight of loneliness. You have no social life. People ask you out, but you have to keep making excuses because you have no one to look after your child and eventually they stop asking. The only people you have a real bond with are other parents who have a child like yours. They understand.

'I spend every evening at home with Yvonne, just the two of us. She's quiet. It's like pulling teeth to get a word out of her or find out what's been happening at the day centre, though she'll talk to her friends if I'm not in the same room. Sometimes she'll get something into her head and repeat it till you are going up the wall. She'll say "Can we have a cat?"

'Now, we've been through this a hundred times before. We can't have a cat because I don't want the responsibility of it at my age, but the people next door have seven and there's usually one of them here. I'll explain all this patiently, and ten minutes later she'll say "Can we have a cat?" It can go on all night. What I'm longing to do is read a book. I can lose myself in a good story, but that would be excluding my daughter, so I just sit there in front of the telly, trying to make a bit of one-sided conversation and feeling a hypocrite.

'I feel sorry for her. I'm sure she finds me dreary company. She used to go to a club sometimes, but I stopped sending her because I used to worry. Sometimes she'd be the first picked up on the minibus and the last dropped off, so she'd be alone with the driver. It's probably a terrible insult to the man, but I couldn't help worrying that something might happen.'

Yvonne attends a day centre and, like many of the older parents, Lilian has been unhappy about recent changes, particularly the move away from providing simple work for a small token wage for students who could cope with it.

Lilian: 'Of course we're not to call them students anymore. It's consumers now apparently. We never know what's going on in the place – there's no liaison. But, I must say, just lately, things have been better. A new man – they used to be called instructors, but I don't know what they are called now – has taken over Yvonne's group, and they now go bowling and to dancing classes. She loves the dancing. She's here getting ready early in the morning, sorting out her money and her packed lunch. It's a great improvement on what she used to do when the changes first started, sitting around looking at magazines. It seems to depend on who's in charge of the group.

'There have been some really silly letters home from the centre. I keep them all in an envelope marked "Nonsense". They're worth looking at for a laugh. There was a timetable including subjects like accounts, numeracy and drama, none of which would mean anything to Yvonne. Then I got a letter home telling me she was to be part of a women's group discussing issues like "different life choices" and "opportunities at different ages". I ask you! If she was capable of understanding things like that I wouldn't have a problem.'

Yvonne is not without her capabilities though. She can see to her personal hygiene but only with supervision. Once, on a weekend away with the centre, nobody reminded her to change her sanitary protection and she came back wearing the towel she went away with. Lilian helps her with bathing and putting on tights: 'I won't let her wear those horrible pop-socks they put on mentally handicapped women in institutions.' She worries about Yvonne's excess weight, and tries, mostly unsuccessfully, to keep her on a diet.

Lilian: 'There are jobs she does well, like polishing and ironing, and she's very bossy. I was on a bus with her once which was full of young schoolchildren messing about, and Yvonne reached over, pushed one of them firmly on to his seat and ordered him to "Sit!" – while I tried to look as if I wasn't with her. I'm sure if she'd been normal, she'd have been an old-fashioned hospital matron, a real dragon, turning perfect corners on beds and terrorizing the nurses and patients.

'There's a funny side to everything, but I've lost my sense of humour lately and my patience. We were out with friends having a meal the other day and I looked across the table at Yvonne and she was quietly picking her nose. I felt so humiliated, I just lost my temper and gave her such a slap.'

Every Saturday Lilian takes Yvonne into town to shop and 'look around'. Days out are arranged during the holidays from the centre, sometimes with a friend and her daughter, who attends the same centre.

Lilian: 'I dread the outings. I'm really not up to them, but I have to find something for Yvonne to do. I haven't enough ironing and polishing to keep her occupied all day.'

The Saturday outings have been made a little easier by some money left to Yvonne by her father. It has been agreed with the Court of Protection, which has charge of her legacy, that they can have a taxi each way.

But the fact that Lilian's ex-husband died suddenly without making a will, caused enormous problems. He owned two properties, one in Ireland, and in the course of the 4 years it took solicitors and estate agents to sell the houses and sort out his affairs, the original sum dwindled from £50,000 to £15,000. The Court of Protection has to be approached for any item Yvonne may need. It also means that she has lost certain government benefits.

Lilian has taken specialist legal advice in making her own will. She has also joined the MENCAP visitors service. For a set sum (currently £3,500) this scheme guarantees a regular visitor for Yvonne after Lilian's death.

Lilian: 'I've made it clear in my will that I want Yvonne to go to a particular home, run by a voluntary organization, when I die. But you have to be realistic. It would be purely coincidence if there was a vacancy there when I died.'

The home in question has offered a place in the near future. Lilian is not sure if she will accept it. There is also an open offer of short-term care. Yvonne has stayed there for a day, but is not keen on going again.

Yvonne: 'I've tried to talk to her into going for a holiday. She says, "I'm thinking about it." But I don't hold out much hope. She used to stay occasionally in another place but they got rid of their short-stay beds and went fully residential. It's very, very hard to get her to agree to leave home even for a few days. I don't even think it's me she's particularly fond of. It's her home she loves.

'I know that if a good place turns up I should snap it up and just make her go, for her sake, but I haven't the courage. If she was easy-going and sociable I'd let her go tomorrow. I envy my friends who have daughters like that.

'But I know exactly what it would be like because she lived away from home for a while when she was a child. That was a lovely place too, but it was miles away and I had no transport. I'd have her home for weekends and she'd be happy till it was time to go back. She'd cry all the way back on the long bus journeys and when I tried to leave her, she'd hang on to me sobbing, and have to be peeled off me by the staff. Sometimes, they admitted, she cried for days. I couldn't go through that again and it would be just the same now. She hasn't changed.'

Thoughts of the future loom large in Lilian's mind. Her normally robust health often lets her down these days.

Lilian: 'Sometimes, when I've been ill, Yvonne will get very worried and say, "You're not going to die, are you?" I reassure her, with more confidence than I feel sometimes. I don't really know what she understands about death. When the parents of friends at the day centre die, she says they've gone to the stars. That's what they taught them at the residential school she used to attend. She seems to know they are not coming back.'

Over the years Lilian has had a series of social workers, and, latterly, community nurses.

Lilian: 'They never seem to stay around long. The best I ever had was a young trainee social worker. He was very left wing, and while I didn't agree with his policies, he really got things done for you. He went off to train and never came back. The woman I have now I hardly ever see. She rang me recently and said she was going to cross me and Yvonne off her list because we didn't have any problems. I wondered how she reached that conclusion. At my age, there are likely to be problems at any time. I told her I didn't want to be crossed off, so apparently I've been put on "hold".'

DOREEN

Thirty-three-year-old Doreen is the youngest of six children. She is relatively able. Her mental handicap wasn't officially acknowledged until she was 12 years old. She was already attending a school for children with special needs – on grounds of her severe epilepsy and a heart condition – and she stayed on there, moving later to an adult training centre.

Unusually, it's Doreen's 68-year-old father, Ralph, who does the talking, not his wife, Betty, who he refers throughout as Mrs H: 'Mrs H has had a series of operations over the years so I have taken over a lot of the caring where Doreen is concerned,' he explained. He is an ex-shop floor worker in the motor industry and now does a lot of voluntary work for people with learning difficulties.

Ralph: 'It was the physical things at first with Doreen; the fits, her heart; a hole in her right eye. They doubted she'd survive into her second year, so even when they told us she had a mental handicap, it wasn't the end of the world. We'd already faced that. The medical people think her mental problems were caused by having bad fits over a long period of time.

'There's a lot Doreen can do now, but that's down to me and Mrs H. If we'd left it to the schools and social services, she'd be sitting around helpless. When she was 14, we made the decision to make her as independent as possible. I came in from work, tired, one night and Mrs H was in a bad mood and there was a big row. We'd been having a lot of rows and I realized it was the tension over Doreen. She wanted this, she wanted that, she wanted waiting on hand and foot and her mother was worn out with it.

'We decided it was time to turn over a new leaf and we started there and then. She had refused to eat what we were having for tea and demanded a boiled egg. I told her if that's what she wanted she could go and cook it herself. She'd seen her mom do it, so she went into the kitchen, put an egg and some water in the saucepan, came out and sat down in front of the telly – and forgot the egg.

'The obvious happened; the water boiled away, the saucepan blackened and there was a terrible smell. We did our best to ignore it, Doreen noticed nothing and in the end we had to remind her. She rushed into the kitchen horrified. She never made the same mistake again.

'We carried on from there. We'd learn her one thing at a time. It was hard work for her and for us, but it had to be done. And there's always an element of risk; you can't remove all the risks from anyone's life, though most parents try to. They over-protect the kids to a ridiculous extent. They won't let them do anything for themselves.

'Doreen can do most things around the house. She keeps her room clean and tidy, she looks after her hygiene, she handles her own money. She gets her own income support and uses it as she pleases, after paying us a bit for her keep. A lot of parents seem to regard their disabled child's allowance as their own. The kids never see it.

'We can go out of the house and leave her on her own for a day, as long as she has a phone number where we can be reached.

'I think the hardest thing we had to teach her was travelling by bus on her own. She used to go on a special bus to her day centre, but I was sure she could manage the normal service which goes from the top of our road. She has a bit of trouble with bus numbers; sometimes seeing them back to front like in dyslexia, so I explained that she was to get the number 35 and she'd know it because it was the one that came round the island.

'It took her a long time to get to the centre that first day, because she stood for two hours at the bus stop before she could get up the confidence to get on. But she made it and now she travels regularly by bus. She knows how to get to and from the college she attends one day each week, and the next route for her to learn will be to our Sandra's.'

Sandra, aged 41, is Doreen's sister. Married, but childless, Ralph says she is the only one of his other children who 'gets on' with Doreen.

Ralph: 'I think maybe we did neglect our other children a bit because we made Doreen a priority. She always needed so much attention. The others aren't so close to her at all, but she and Sandra have always been great friends, and a few years ago, Sandra said she and her husband would have Doreen when we're gone. It came out of the blue.

'Me and Mrs H never expected the other children to be responsible for her but I must admit it's a great relief. It's made us even more determined that she should be independent, because Sandra and her husband have a very free lifestyle, having no children of their own, and it wouldn't be fair if Doreen spoiled that for them.

'I used to think I'd like her to live in a flat of her own one day, but then I started doing a bit of voluntary driving, delivering furniture to people in that position and I was put off by what I saw. The state of some of those flats! In one there was a big pile of dirty washing in the corner of the living room and a burn on a carpet which the girl said had been caused by her electric blanket. It made you wonder what it had done to the bed!

'A social worker called in once a week and it just wasn't enough. These people can get very isolated. Thank God Doreen won't have to go through that.'

Ralph and Betty have very little time for social workers, or other outside help.

Ralph: 'We had a social worker once, for 18 months, and she caused more problems than she solved. She persuaded us to let Doreen go to a hostel for respite care, but it was just around the corner and if anything upset her – which often happened – she'd just come home. They wouldn't give her a place further away.

'She stopped going after something happened there that upset her badly. She came home very distressed and refused to go back, but she wouldn't tell us what was wrong, and the staff never gave us any explanation. She's never been back. It's her choice. We wouldn't make her do what she didn't want to.

'I agree with this self-advocacy, teaching them to stand on their own two feet and say what they want. But if they have the right to say "yes", they also have the right to say "no". For instance, we went to a talk on sexuality and people with a mental handicap, at which the idea put forward was that you should teach them all about sex, even if they weren't showing any interest. That seems ridiculous to me. Why create a problem? Doreen learned all she needs to know about menstruation and that, but she's never shown any interest in sex. Just the opposite. She'll hold her mother's hand and kiss her – or Sandra – but if any man comes near her or touches her, she'll push him away.

'Maybe she'll change. If she does we'll cross that bridge when we come to it. For the moment, it seems to me that she's saying "no" – and we'll defend her right to go on saying it.'

GETTING HELP

Caresearch

A computer-based system which matches up a person with a mental handicap with the most suitable residential places available. It works rather like a dating agency, with parent or a professional who knows the handicapped person filling in a detailed questionnaire, and the computer coming up with an address or addresses. The family and/or social worker take it from there. There is a small fee.

The only family I interviewed who had tried the scheme had received just one address – but they were trying to place two profoundly multi-handicapped adults together:
c/o United Response,
Kew Bridge House,
Kew Bridge Road ,
Brentford,
Middlesex TW8 0ED.
Tel: 081-847 3971.

Trustee Visitors Service

Undertakes to provide a visitor who will take an interest in a person with a mental handicap after his/her parents' death. You join by making a single payment, entering into a deed of covenant or making provision in a will: MENCAP (see general addresses section p.183).

General Support

An older carer needs all the practical help he/she can muster. Try tracking down the following in your area:

Bath nurse – A nursing auxilliary who can give help with bathing a handicapped person. Contact via the GP.

Community Nurse – In some areas the mental handicap community nurse will provide 'hands on' physical help such as bathing and dressing a person with a handicap, but their role varies from place to place. Contact: GP or Social Services.

Home Help (sometimes now called home care assistants) – Many local authorities will provide a family who have a member with a disability with help once a week or so. Again the home help's duties vary from housework to a near-nursing role, depending on the area.

Contact: The home help or home care organizer at the Social Services department.

Occupational Therapist – Aids to help the person with a handicap (or indeed the elderly carer) around the house. Can also provide advice on adapting the home. Contact: Social Services department.

Care Attendant – If there is such a scheme in your area, it might be run by a voluntary group or the local authority. The idea is to send a trained person into the home to give the carer a break, or to help with duties like getting the disabled person bathed or dressed or ready for a day centre in the morning. Some schemes also provide a night-sitter to give the parents at least an occasional good night's sleep if it is normally disrupted. The bad news is that they don't exist everywhere and they tend to have waiting lists. Contacts: Social Services Department, your GP or

The Association of Crossroads Care Attendant Schemes,
10 Regent Place,
Rugby,
Warwickshire CV21 2PN.
Tel: 0788 73653.

5 The Other Children

There's a widely-held belief that a handicapped child makes for a handicapped family, and though many parents would disagree, there's no doubt that growing up alongside a brother or sister with a mental handicap affects your life. Not all the effects are bad. Some adult siblings will tell you that they are better people for the experience – less selfish, more tolerant, more mature and more aware and intuitive, as a result of dealing with someone who cannot easily make their needs understood.

But that's looking at it with hindsight. From a child's point of view it can be hard to understand why a handicapped brother gets away with behaviour that would merit a major punishment for you; why he's allowed to take up so much of your mother's time that there's little left over for you and why you are expected to look after someone who's bigger and older than yourself, and generally act like a little grown-up when it suits the real grown-ups.

Life outside the family is hard to come to terms with too, where adults may stare and other children make fun of your brother and tease you about him. Even when friends are sympathetic and sensible, taking them home can be an ordeal if your sibling is likely to behave in an odd fashion or is incontinent. And on top of it all is the guilt at feeling this way. After all, you're the lucky one. How can you be jealous of or embarrassed by someone who, through no fault of their own, will never be able to do a fraction of the things you can?

Pauline Fairbrother who, under the umbrella of MENCAP, set up the organization SIBS (it stands for siblings, but also for Support and Information for Brothers and Sisters) has learned a lot about the feelings of the other children. She has three grown-up daughters, of whom Diana, the middle one, has a mental handicap. She has always been aware that growing up with Diana made life more complicated for her other daughters – particularly the youngest, Ruth.

In 1979 Pauline met Janet Baiter, who had two brothers with

mental handicap. Janet, then 20, had left home to go to college. She loved her new life and the freedom it offered, but every time she went home for a weekend, she was overwhelmed by guilt at having left her parents to cope without her. The pull between what she felt was her duty and the independent life she wanted was making her miserable, and Janet felt sure there must be others like herself. Wouldn't it be possible, she asked in a letter to MENCAP, to set up self-help therapy groups, where adult siblings like herself could talk out their confused feelings? Her letter was directed to Pauline.

From their meeting the newsletter SIBS was born, followed by the groups Janet wanted. At these meetings, Pauline says:

> Floodgates were opened. Memories locked up inside poured out, were examined, talked about, laughed or cried over and finally laid to rest or at least understood. Afterwards some people were able to talk to their parents for the first time about how they had felt as children and how they felt as adults. Their parents were often shocked, but it led to a much greater understanding of each other.

SIBS runs workshops for young brothers and sisters, where they can talk, and often act out their feelings and experiences:

> It can be unintentionally hilarious. You'll have a child describing something like how often his sister is sick, and another child will say his brother spits all the time, and a third will chip in with, "I bet my brother spits more than yours." It's probably the first time they've really talked about the nitty-gritty of life with their handicapped sibling, because they are with other children, who understand and won't be shocked.

The contributions in the newsletters are sometimes sad and often sensible. A 14-year-old writes, 'I used to think how nice it would be if I had a normal brother and our family was normal. But after a while I realized that everyone thought their families were weird.'

Another, writing about the birth of her handicapped sister says, 'When my sister came home I kept on crying. It took me six weeks to get over it. When I got back to school all my friends said, 'Did your mother have her baby?' I said 'yes'. It took me about two weeks to tell my friends.'

Then there's the girl who dashed home from school, all excited, to tell her mother she'd got all A-grades in her report. 'And she [her mother] says, "Oh, that's nice. Guess what? Your brother said so-and-so today" and went on and on about it. That really hurt me.'

What can parents do to help? Pauline Fairbrother advises them, first and foremost, just to be aware of their other child's feelings and possible difficulties inside and outside the home. Children should be encouraged to express their feelings, good and bad; given some special time for themselves when possible, and always reassured of their parents' love. She believes that parents should give them all the information on their brother or sister's condition that they can understand – leaflets or books (particularly stories which feature a child with a similar disability) can help them explain to their friends.

OTHER EXPERIENCES

One of the cruellest problems the families I spoke to had to deal with was the mockery of other children. One mother described what her 6-year-old son went through after fellow-pupils saw his 3-year-old severely handicapped brother.

> They'd taunt him in the playground – 'Your brother dribbles, your brother's a spastic' – all the nasty names would come out. I spoke to his teacher and asked if she would point out to them that David was unlucky having a brother with a handicap and that they should be sympathetic instead of unkind. It seemed to work – or David just learned to put up with it. He doesn't like telling tales and he's had to grow up quickly anyway.

Maureen talked about the way a group of boys would dance round her son, Steven, after they'd seen his handicapped brother, chanting, 'cabbage'. 'I went to see the mother of the ringleader but nothing came of it. She didn't manage to stop her son. It eventually died out of its own accord.'

Helen, whose young son was also taunted about his older brother, approached the school: 'They were very good. They devised an assembly about handicapped children and Andrew talked about his brother. It made all the difference and the teachers said they were glad I'd told them about my handicapped son because it helped them understand Andrew better and be aware of his feelings.'

However, according to Judith, no amount of intervention worked for her daughter, so she devised an unusual plan. 'My daughter had a very bad time at school because of her brother, and she was falling behind academically because his behaviour was so unruly she couldn't get any school work done at home.'

Judith's controversial solution, as her local authority could not find a suitable day centre for her son, was to ask them to fund her daughter's education at a good boarding school instead: 'I saw it as a wonderful opportunity for her to get a good education and get away from the havoc her brother created.'

The outcome has not been all Judith hoped for. Her daughter, who recently graduated at university, feels 'that she was pushed out, rejected, so that her brother could stay at home. She's very resentful, which I can't understand because she enjoyed her time at boarding school, and it was definitely for her own good.'

Many parents mentioned how quickly their non-handicapped children had to grow up because they simply didn't have time to 'baby' them. This is particularly noticeable with a child who is younger than the sibling with a handicap, who has probably always had to do more for himself or herself and accept more responsibility than his or her peers.

It is also the youngest who feels the restrictions most keenly. Too young to go out without a parent, especially during school holidays, they are confined to home while their friends are taken on spur-of-the-moment outings whenever the sun shines. Planning an outing with a child who has a handicap can be like masterminding a major assault. Spontaneity is the first casualty. If the child has a multiple handicap, it is often just impossible for brothers and sisters ever to enjoy the out-of-home treats. It's also pretty difficult to get them to the dentist or buy a new pair of shoes!

This was one of the reasons that, along with 2 other mothers, I founded the Birmingham Multi-Handicap Group, catering for the most profoundly handicapped children and adults living at home. This small group, set up on a grant from the Inner City Partnership, with a co-ordinator housed in someone's spare room, has grown to a major respite care service, copied in many other areas.

It provides trained and paid care assistants who go into the family home and take over the care of the handicapped person while parents take a break. What they do with the break is up to them. They can go out for an evening, go away for a weekend, or take a very frustrated small sister on the outings her friends took for granted – which is what I used to do.

Bringing friends home can also be a porblem for brothers and sisters, though most parents say that their normal children's close friends have been marvellous with the handicapped sibling. Occasionally, newcomers react in unexpected ways. One teenage girl explained:

> My friends used to act very casual at first but they'd go all quiet and strange when they heard Peter moving about the house. He doesn't walk very well and he makes a lot of noise. It took me ages to realize that they were actually frightened of him. I had to explain that when he shuffled up to them he wasn't going to hurt them, he only wanted to be friendly. I think some of them found it hard to react in a natural way with him; they were always a bit self-conscious about how they should behave. When you've known him all your life it's quite hard to see your brother through someone else's eyes.

A little later on, there's likely to be the boyfriend or girlfriend to introduce. Most adult siblings were adamant that they would never go out with the sort of person who didn't get on with their handicapped brother or sister. As one 18-year-old put it: 'If a girl was put off by my brother I wouldn't think much of her. It's a kind of test really, to see if a girl is the right one for me!'

Parents often deny that the child with the handicap caused any problems to the others, but you do wonder if they just haven't noticed. It took Harry, now in his seventies, a long time.:

> Looking back, our eldest lad must have been embarrassed by his brother when they were teenagers. At that age being different, in any way, is the end of the world, isn't it? He wasn't the sort who'd tell you his troubles and we didn't think about it at the time . . . always too busy struggling with our own problems, I suppose.

On the other hand, there are siblings who will vouch for the fact that they felt no ill-effects from the experience. I asked 22-year-old Matthew (his sister, Anita, is interviewed in this section p.167) what it had been like growing up with Nick, his younger brother who has Down's Syndrome: 'No problem,' he said. 'He was just like anyone else's younger brother. I don't even remember he's handicapped most of the time.'

An interview with his mother, Joan, proved this was no exaggeration:

> Matt recently brought home his new girlfriend from university, and when Nick walked into the room I saw this expression of surprise, even shock, on her face. She covered it well and she was fine with Nick, but I was horrified because I've told Matt ever since he was a little boy to explain to friends about Nick before he brings them home. It's a courtesy thing really. When I got him alone I said,
>
> 'You didn't tell her about Nick, did you?'
>
> 'Tell her what?' he said.
>
> 'That he has Down's Syndrome,' I said.
>
> 'Oh, that,' he said. 'Sorry, I didn't think of it.'

Compare that with Jacqueline, interviewed below, whose life as a child and adult has revolved around the needs of her younger brother. If it proves anything, it's that you can't generalize.

SPEAKING FOR THEMSELVES

JACQUELINE

Jacqueline (29) is the only sibling of Carl (25), whose mother is interviewed in the 'Young Adults' section of this book (p.125). Jacqueline works in an office. Her father, a self-employed car mechanic, died recently. They live in a modern council house in the outer suburbs of a city.

Jacqueline: 'Nobody explained about Carl's problems when I was a child, as far as I can remember. But I used to go to his hospital appointments with my mother, so I knew something was wrong. I just accepted it, I suppose, the same way I accepted that I was expected to share the burden of looking after him.

'The feeling that he was my responsibility was always there. For years and years I could never go out on a Saturday because I had to look after Carl. There's a lot of common land and parks around here, so I used to take him out. Sometimes my best friend came with me. Other kids would laugh at him and take the mickey, but you get so used to it you take no notice. You don't think about it deeply when you're young – is this fair? Am I being put upon? It becomes a way of life.

'I still take Carl out with Mum every Saturday when he's at home. He goes away now some weekends and I really look forward to those. My social life is planned around them. If I want to go on a coach trip or something with the girls from work, it has to be on those weekends. The same with a holiday – I take mine during the week Carl is away.

'Dad dying didn't make any difference to the amount of time I spend with Carl. He was never home anyway. It's always been mine and Mum's job. She's better at coping with him now; she couldn't cope at all when he was young. I don't know how she'd manage if I wasn't there.

'Carl is very, very hard work. He's always on the go, into everything. He's an inquisitive 3-year-old in a man's body. Up until 12 years ago, he shared a bedroom with me because our grandfather lived here, I never had a private place where I could keep my things safely or take friends.

'I've never brought friends home much anyway. I've only ever had one or two close friends, people who accept Carl. Just recently I broke up with the boyfriend I've been going out with for a long time, which is a shame because he was great with Carl.

'I pick my friends very carefully. I don't mention Carl until I get to know someone well. Then I explain what he's like. I think people shy away from coming into contact with anyone mentally handicapped because they expect something grotesque. But Carl looks quite nice and he's a very loving person, like a little boy. I've never had anyone run out in horror, but it can still be embarrassing. It's not like going into a house where there is no Carl.

'When I was a child I used to wish I could meet other kids like myself. I used to think "I'm the only person in the world with a Carl." You feel like an outsider. The other kids don't understand what your life is like. I love my brother, but sometimes I resent him – and I resent my mother for pressing me into this mould where I feel so responsible I'm trapped. When I think about the things I could have done with my life – travelled abroad, met lots of different people – I feel bitter. I feel like packing my bags and running away, but of course, I won't.

'If I do leave home, I'll have to live nearby and carry on helping with Carl. When Mum dies or is unable to look after him, I'll take over full-time. I'd like to get married but any future husband would have to be willing to live with Carl. As for having children of my own, I'm not sure. It's not that I'm frightened of having one with a handicap – Carl's condition is not genetic – but I just wouldn't have the time to devote to a family. Carl takes up so much of my life.'

ANITA

Twenty-four-year-old Anita, recently married, works in a bank. She is the eldest of three children. The youngest of her two brothers, 17-year-old Nick, has Down's Syndrome. Her mother, Joan, is quoted in the 'Finding Out' section of the book (p. 18).

Anita: 'I don't remember Mum and Dad ever sitting down with us and telling us formally about Nick's handicap, but it was always talked about openly. There wasn't a lot of noticeable difference between him and any other baby at first. He was a very enjoyable, happy little child – far less of a nuisance than my other brother!

'But Nick could be hard work. I taught him to climb the stairs and it took ages. I remember thinking, "If this takes a long time, how long is it going to take him to learn other things?" I suppose I realized around that time that he really was different.

'He's always been very much the baby of the family, and he still is. I sometimes think my mother is not firm enough with him. For instance, he hates getting up in the morning and she spends ages every day trying to persuade him to get up and get dressed for the school transport. I tell her to put him on the bus in his pyjamas. It would soon cure him.

'I do sympathize with him about not wanting to go to school though. It's a waste of time for him. He's been there since he was 5, he's bored and boredom makes him idle. Yet if you involve him in things he likes, he'll be really interested. It's like that with pop music. He's a real expert on the subject. He and I are quite alike in some ways. The rest of the family are sports enthusiasts, but me and Nick prefer music and films and television.

'I'd have liked his school to involve me more when I was younger and living at home. I could have picked up what they were trying to teach him and done it with him. My parents go to the school, but I don't think brothers and sisters are invited. Nick's much brighter than a lot of the children there. Being with them all the time drags him down. He's a great mimic and if he was with brighter children he'd act more like them.

'The school sends him and some others out to a nearby comprehensive for some periods each week and the kids there, some of them very rough, really accept him. In the street you hear kids shouting, "You mongol" at each other – I'm sure they are not among the ones who have been introduced to kids with mental handicap or learning difficulties in their schools. But I'm not sure about proper integration, putting him in a classroom with normal children. I mean, he couldn't do any of the work they do, though he can read a bit and write his name now. You know what I really think would have made a massive difference to Nick? A private tutor, someone to come in every day and work with him alone. I think he'd be doing amazing things if he'd had that.

'I've never been embarrassed by him. I can take him anywhere, introduce him to anyone and trust him to behave properly. It never crossed my mind that my schoolfriends or boyfriends would find him unacceptable or peculiar. I'd often tell people about him without mentioning that he has a handicap. You're so used to it yourself that you almost forget it. It's like this "rrr-ing" noise. He makes this tuneless, repetitive sound a lot and visitors will start looking around and asking "What's that noise?" We don't even notice it till someone points it out. At my wedding I'm sure there were people from Malcolm's side of the family who wondered about him but I've never felt the need to explain him to anyone. He's so friendly people just like him for what he is.

'The only times I've resented Nick was when we were younger and he always seemed to get away with things while I got told off. But you can't tell him off – if you are annoyed with him he gets so upset, it isn't worth it. It's the same with family rows. If he sees any of us angry with each other he becomes very upset and disturbed. It means you always have to control your temper. We've never been able to have a real, stand-up row, and that was very hard when I was a teenager.

'One of the funny things is that people think if you have a child in the family with a mental handicap you are wonderful with all handicapped people. It's just not true. On one of the few occasions I've been in Nick's school, there was this child who kept leaning over me and she dribbled badly. I just didn't know what to do. I was sort of transfixed. Nick came up and, ever so gently, moved her away. "Please don't dribble on my sister," he said.

'Nothing ruffles Nick. As long as he has his records, his television and his video tapes, and an evening out at the Gateway club for mentally handicapped people once each week, he's happy. I certainly don't feel sorry for him. If I feel sorry for anyone it's my parents who will always have a child to look after even when they're old. I do feel a certain amount of responsibility for him, of course, but our parents don't expect me or my other brother to take him into our homes when they are gone.

'Where will he live? Well, he can look after himself in a limited way – he can cook beans on toast and make tea – but he needs a lot of supervision. He tends to cut himself off in his own little world unless there are people around to stimulate him and take an interest in him. He could even do a little job but he has this problem with his eyes, which would make it hard for him to get buses or travel anywhere except on special transport. I don't really know what will happen in the future, but I'm sure that wherever he goes, there will always be people around who will like Nick. People do; he's a nice person.'

HUGH

Now 44 and a social worker, Hugh is the second eldest of four children. The youngest, 36-year-old Madelaine, has a mental handicap. Hugh is divorced.

Hugh: 'I can be very glib now and say what should have happened. My parents should have explained to the rest of us exactly what Madelaine's problems were and what the situation was. But for that to happen they would have had to be working together and agreed on what the reality was – in fact my father never really accepted that my sister had a handicap. Even when she had to be transferred from mainstream to special education at the age of 5 he still cherished a hope that she would magically make a giant leap and catch up.

'He overprotected her totally. She was never controlled and so these terrible infantile tantrums she used to have carried on as she grew up. Yet when she was older, it became obvious that she had substantial ability if it had been developed. She learned to read and moved into a group home, where she coped pretty well. I'm sure that if she'd been handled more firmly and encouraged to have more self-control as a child she'd have been quite an able adult. But my father wouldn't let her grow up.

'The effect Madelaine's arrival had on our family was to put it into cold storage. The normal evolution of the family, whereby the children grow up and leave home and the parents revert to being a couple again never happened. Because my sister was always there my parents never did become a couple.

'I feel that they tried to keep us, the other children, at the stage the family was in when Madelaine was born. Certainly they hung on to all of us. It was very hard to leave home, because you knew you were leaving them with the difficult job of bringing my sister up in isolation. I suspect one of the reasons I got married was to have an excuse to leave. I felt particularly bad about my mother. It was her who shouldered most of the work and there was a great deal of tension between her and my father. I can remember him coming home from work and my mother trying to tell him what a hard day she'd had and what Madelaine had done and he'd just turn away. He didn't want to know.

'I can't remember a time at which I first became aware my sister was limited. I can't remember being told or discussing it with my brother and sister, but it's well known that people who have had a disrupted childhood often have great gaps in their memory.

'All our mother's time and energy, and most of our father's, went into Madelaine. Her learning difficulty wasn't the problem, her behaviour was. If she wanted something she had to have it or she went berserk. She had no control and she was always given in to. My strongest overall memory is of the stress of everyday living and of wanting to make things right but not knowing how.

'Madelaine is now at home with my mother again. She was living in a group home but when my father became ill, she started spending more time at home. When he died my mother was lonely and she had Madelaine back to live at home. I don't think it's the best place for her. When my mother dies, though hopefully that won't be for a long time, Madelaine will have two major traumas to face – not only the loss of the person closest to her, but having to move to a new home.

'I've kept in close touch with Madelaine, but I would never have her to live with me. She won't ever be even semi-independent and I've always accepted that I will play a role in her life – visiting her, taking her out, seeing she is comfortable and well-cared for. I don't resent it. It's my responsibility.'

GETTING HELP

SIBS(Support and Information for Brothers and Sisters)

Produces a members' newsletter and can provide information and guidelines for setting up groups. There are two videos, 'The Other Children' and 'We Were The Other Children', aimed at professionals working with families, but also of interest to parents and brothers and sisters. The SIBS editorial office is at MENCAP National Centre (addresses in General Addresses section).

BOOKS

One of the recognized ways for young brothers and sisters to understand their handicapped sibling's problems and come to terms with their own feelings is through reading about families in their own position. Most children's librarians will be able to advise on what's appropriate. Look out for the following: 'The Four of Us' by E. Beresford (1981, Hutchinson), 'My Brother Barry' by B. Gillham (1981, Andre Deutsch) 'Ben' by V. Shennan (1980, Bodley Head) and 'The Bus People' by R. Anderson (1989, Oxford University Press).

6 Alternatives

For almost every condition there's a conventional treatment and an alternative, often controversial method. The two widely-discussed alternatives where children with physical and mental disability are concerned, are the Doman-Delacato 'patterning' method, used at the Institute for the Achievement of Human Potential in the United States, and Conductive Education, pioneered at the Peto Institute of Hungary.

Both have their followers and detractors. The medical profession in particular likes to see hard academic evidence before grudgingly taking anything slightly 'different' under its wing. Parents aren't too bothered about the technical studies. They know of a child doing well on the programme, they read a few success stories in the papers and are willing to beg, borrow and possibly steal, to pay for treatment for their child. Certainly many parents have become expert fundraisers in order to raise the cost of trips to Hungary or America before any help was available here.

Rarely do they embark on such a venture with stars in their eyes. 'It's a chance, nothing more, nothing less', explained a father about to start his child on the Doman-Delacato programme. 'You owe it to your child to give him that chance. What have you got to lose and what's the alternative? For my child, a life in a wheelchair, ending up in some institution.'

But is he right? Isn't there actually a lot a family has to lose by committing themselves to a demanding, long-term régime, concentrated on one child? And is the gloomy alternative based in reality? Isn't there much that can be achieved by conventional treatment and modern attitudes towards handicap? And most importantly of all – do the treatments work? Unfortunately there's no easy answer. Parents have to make up their own minds.

PATTERNING

The Kerland Child Development Centre was established in 1982 and moved into it's smart new, purpose-built clinic (opened by Honorary President Joan Collins) in Somerset in 1986. It was an off-shoot of the British Institute for Brain Injured Children, where some of it's staff trained. The British Institute, itself originally modelled on the parent Institute in Philadelphia, usually prescribes full-day courses of home treatment. The Kerland Centre had modified this, and feels that as much can be achieved by parents working around 3 hours each day with the child, which does not necessitate taking her or him out of school. Some schools agree to continue the child's programme in the classroom, but most families have to fit it in before school and in the evenings. They also have to recruit a team of friends and neighbours to come in and help.

The Doman-Delacato patterning method is basically an intensive programme of stimulation for brain-damaged children, which takes them back to the earliest stages of development by teaching them to crawl. It works on the principle that we only use 10 per cent of our brain cells in a lifetime, and that the 90 per cent spare capacity can be trained to take over the work of the damaged cells. It's the logic of this theory that is so convincing to parents.

Children attend the clinic, which is fee-paying, for an initial 2 days of assessment (and training for parents). They return at intervals of 4–6 months for reassessment and adjustments to their child's personal programme. The programme will certainly include patterning – where the child's arms and legs are moved through the motions of crawling by 3 or 4 people.

There will probably also be 'masking' sessions, involving a plastic mask being placed briefly over the nose and mouth of the child to make his breathing deeper. He may be swung by two people holding arms and legs, hung upside down, made to hang by his hands from a horizontal ladder over his head and encouraged to swing along on this, hand over hand. This involves families finding space in their home for bulky equipment. Outside of all this there is tactile stimulation, exercises for ears and eyes and flashcards.

Some children enjoy the programme, others object strongly to parts of it. Six-year-old Tommy from Belgium, who was there for reassessment the day I visited, was terrified of the mask over his face. The therapist decided to try something else. He was placed on a padded patterning table in the gymnasium-cum-treatment room and a corset-like garment with straps fixed around his chest.

One person stood on each side of the table, pulling and releasing the straps, which had the effect of making Tommy breathe deeply without any effort on his part. He loved it, giggling at the new game. After a good start, Tommy had only made a little progress in the last 6 months and his mother had met with discouragement from the medical profession. But she saw changes and wanted to continue.

The centre treats a range of problems caused by brain damage, of which mental handicap is just one. Their literature says: 'We cannot guarantee progress at all but many children are today enjoying a far better quality of life that their parents ever dared imagined.' It's a modest claim. I suspect that experts studying what they call 'sensorimotor patterning' in the past have been irritated by the far greater claims made by the American Institute, where the method originated.

Research, on the whole, has been limited and negative. One group went so far as to describe the programme as 'useless, expensive and possibly harmful'. Others however have recorded improvements in language and self-help skills. Many noted a great spurt in development during the first 3 months, but found that it tailed off considerably by 6 and particularly 9 months.

This ties in with my own personal experience. Between the ages of 3½ and 6, my son, Patrick, was on a Doman-Delacato programme. Every morning and afternoon, 3 or 4 helpers arrived to put Patrick through his paces on the patterning table and on the floor. Very quickly he went from being totally immobile to crawling. He began to sit better, to look at books, to recognize numbers and pictures on flashcards. Then, gradually, his progress slowed and stopped. At this point, as researchers have noted with other families, came the guilt. Had I not worked hard enough? Had I allowed the new baby to blunt my determination? Should I have carried on, anyway, regardless?

I don't regret the years spent on the programme. My alternative in those days was to sit and watch, day after day, a child who did nothing. There were no child development centres, no welcoming schools at the age of 2 and there is nothing more frustrating than wanting desperately to help and no knowing how. The programme kept me sane.

But it is hard work and it can cause family arguments if both parents are not equally committed. There's also the extra bit of guilt about neglecting the other children. How families with several children manage to do it – even a reduced programme – is beyond me. But they do and they get results. Whatever the researchers turn up, I've never known a child who didn't improve on it, but on the other hand, I've never known a total success story either.

KIERON

Apart from a couple of breaks, 6-year-old Kieron has been on the Kerland programme for nearly 3 years. His mother, Julie, says he had made dramatic progress, but admits that over 3 hours of intensive exercises and stimulation per day is stressful and can have a worrying effect on the other children.

When I spoke to her, the family were taking a 4-month break from treatment because Kieron's 3-year-old sister, Michelle, had become so disturbed by his crying during the exercise sessions.

Julie: 'We've explained to her that what we are doing is for Kieron's good, but she's too young to understand. She's started screaming and hitting out at the volunteers who come in to help. We want to do everything possible for Kieron, but not at the expense of our other two children, so we're stopping till Michelle goes to school. Fortunately my 7-year-old son understands and we keep him involved in everything that's going on.'

Kieron has a rare brain condition which makes it hard for him to coordinate both sides of his brain. It affects him physically and mentally, leaving him with multiple handicaps. Julie recalls, with horror, the poor prognosis given when he was a baby.

Julie: 'The doctor more or less told us he'd be a vegetable. The words he used were, "He's a freak of nature". I thought, "He may be a freak to you but to us he's our little boy". It made me ten times more determined to help Kieron.'

But the combined efforts of a physiotherapist and staff at the school where Kieron started at 2½ had little effect on his development.

When Julie and her husband saw the Kerland Centre and it's treatment mentioned on a television news programme they decided, 'It made such good sense, we had to try it.'

The initial assessment costs them £320, plus the cost of 2 nights in a hotel, and travel. They were immediately impressed by what they saw.

Julie: 'It's a lovely, homely place and the staff were so encouraging, after the awful things we'd been told. When we left we really believed we could achieve a lot with Kieron – and we were right.

'It took just 3 months to change him from a totally helpless baby who could only just roll over to an alert little boy with his own personality. He could recognize pictures. If you held up flashcards of a train and a dog and asked which was the dog, he'd reach out for the right picture. He has continued to improve. He feeds himself and, though he has very little balance, he can walk if you hold his hand.'

They do the exercises before and after school, difficult times for voluntary helpers. The helpers responded to a piece in the local paper and on local radio. 'It wasn't easy, but it wasn't impossible,' Julie says. 'We've managed to get 20 regulars, and others who found they couldn't come at the right time decided to help by fundraising.'

The money was needed to pay for reassessments and to build equipment, most of which a carpenter friend made cheaply. There's a pulley system in the living room, from which Kieron is suspended, first right way up, then upside down. There's also an 8-foot-long overhead ladder, and Julie's sewing machine table, opened out and padded, works as a patterning table.

The hardest thing to deal with has been the fact that Keiron dislikes parts of the programme and protests loudly each session.

Julie: 'You just have to harden yourself to him crying because you know it's for his own good. But I do get ever so depressed hearing him, especially if I have to do every session. It's better if I have enough patterners to let them to get on with it themselves and I leave the room and do something else.'

CONDUCTIVE EDUCATION

Most of the recent publicity surrounding Conductive Education sprang from families in the country raising money to take their children to the Peto Institute in Hungary for treatment, and from the subsequent opening of the Birmingham Institute for Conductive Education. This centre treats a number of young day pupils with cerebral palsy, but doesn't take children with a mental handicap, so need not concern us here.

What is more relevant is the work based on Conductive Education principles that the Spastics Society is doing in its schools, and the fact that the Society has 12 students at the Peto Institute training to be conductors (the term used for the multi-faceted teachers who combine the duties of therapist, teacher nurse and care staff).

The controversy attached to this method arose from a feeling among professionals that parents were grasping it as a miracle cure, suitable for every child with a physical disability. Physiotherapists, one of the professions whose jobs would be usurped by conductors, accuse the Conductive Education proponents of raising false hopes by making exaggerated claims. They also criticize the regimented nature of the system, which, they say, demands that children adapt to suit the treatment rather than the other way round. Others complain of the 'choosiness' of a system that treats only those it thinks will do well.

The Spastics Society has been incorporating aspects of the system in some of its schools since the 1960s, but following the present wave of publicity, it has been strongly criticized for calling this Conductive Education when staff had not been through the 4-year training. It's been criticized for opposing the system and not taking steps to introduce it to Britain in its pure form. The Society now says that it was never against Conductive Education, only certain individuals within the organization expressed doubts, and it is now committed to using it and opening new outreach centres, which will bring it to many more children.

It still cautions, however, that this 'is just one of a number of therapies which is suitable for some children. It is not suitable for everyone and is not a cure for their condition but may enable them to overcome their disorders and function more independently.'

RUTLAND HOUSE

Carol Oviatt-Ham, headteacher of the Spastics Society's Rutland House residential school in Nottingham, has been using Conductive Education principles with children with cerebral palsy and severe multiple learning difficulties for 14 years. She has no doubt it works for them, nor have the parents of her pupils whose £27,500 annual fees are paid for by their local authorities.

Mrs Oviatt-Ham has studied with Ester Cotton, the physiotherapist who introduced the Peto method to this country in 1965, and has been to the Institute of Budapest.

'The Institute was treating only children with normal intellectual ability, but I thought the principles could be applied to those with multiple handicaps and severe learning difficulties. When I got this job it was my opportunity to prove it.'

The argument against using Conductive Education with children who have a mental handicap is that it is a learning process and calls for them to understand and follow instructions. But Carol Oviatt-Ham says that her children do come to understand as long as the same language is used consistently:

We also use sign language and pictures. The great advantage of this system for these children is that every lesson, treatment and activity is carried out in the same group, by the same people, in the same setting. What happens normally is that their lives are fragmented. They go to school for lessons, somewhere different to see a paediatrician, somewhere else for physiotherapy – and few of these people know the whole child or what he or she is able to do.

We, on the other hand, are looking at the whole child, developing the whole personality. Inside the most damaged body and brain, there is a child trying to get out. We refuse to accept that any child is a hopeless case, and, thank goodness, parents today are refusing to take a damning diagnosis from a doctor as gospel. They are seeking other sources of help.

At Rutland House, the whole day, from waking to sleeping, is one long learning opportunity. The children are divided into groups of around six. Each child has a dressing and washing programme, followed by breakfast, then they sit at a plinth – the slatted table, which along with the ladder-backed chair, makes up the essential equipment of Conductive Education – with their feet firmly on the floor, head straight up, eyes ahead as they feed themselves or are fed. Sometimes there is a mirror in front of them so that they can watch the process and learn from it.

After breakfast comes a 2-hour motor (movement) programme around the plinth. Everything starts with the hand. Children are encouraged to open their often tightly-coiled fingers. If they can hold the slats in the plinth they can sit alone and also pull themselves up. Getting them to sit up is the first step to developing all sorts of other skills. In that position they can see what is happening, see what they're doing themselves in a mirror, hold a spoon or a toy, make eye contact and begin to communicate.

Those who cannot sit may wear a splint or a brace or be held in that position. Exercises are repeated over and over, with the therapist and, if possible, the child chanting the action as they perform it. When a child can't do the movements, the therapist, one to each child, takes him through the motions. One of the staff said: 'To the children it's like a physical workout – and you know how good that can make you feel.'

Certainly it's thirsty work. Afterwards there's time for a drink, still seated at the plinth. Then there is toileting. No nappies here – the children sit on their pots for as long as it takes and most become potty-trained.

After lunch, they have the opportunity for a rest on the plinth. This too is part of therapy. They are positioned for the maximum benefit to their particular disability, with a splint holding a leg or a hand in position if needed. The afternoon brings more groups activities – they are divided into groups according to age and ability – and school finishes at 4.30 pm. The school works to its own terms – six weeks on, two weeks off, with most of the children going home for holidays.

THE NURSERY

Down in the day nursery, fitted out, of course, with plinths and ladder-backed chairs, there are a dozen or so under-5s, accompanied by their mothers. This is a scheme which opens up Conductive Education, at no cost, to any family with a young child with cerebral palsy who can get to Nottingham. Its days are as tightly-packed as the school's, with the difference that here the mothers are on duty to help.

The unit is open every weekday for 43 weeks of the year. There are 50 children on the books, each coming in for 2 to 4 days of the week. They come from the surrounding counties, and from as far afield as Hampshire and Wales. Some parents stay nearby overnight to pack in two consecutive days. Carol Oviatt-Ham likes to get the children as early as possible. They can start at 6 months, though most are older.

'Little children are easier to work with,' she says. 'They haven't learned to be handicapped.' She feels that the nursery educates the parents too.

Often, in the early days, parents don't actually understand what is wrong with their child. Many of them have had a chilling prognosis, suggesting that the child will be severely handicapped and never do anything. Most of those you'll see sitting up in chairs eating their lunch have parents who have been told they will never sit up. Probably the greatest support mothers get here comes from other mothers. A new mum may say she's been told her child will never do anything and one of the others will say, 'Oh yes, they said that about mine too, but look at him now!'

BEN

Sheila has been bringing her only child, 3-year-old Ben, to the Rutland Nursery four times a week for 2 years. She drives over, a 45-minute journey, and believes Ben has benefited greatly. 'But I'm under no illusions. We still have a long way to go. He's not sitting up yet, but he's more aware and his head control is brilliant compared to the way it used to be.'

Ben has been diagnosed as having cerebral palsy, epilepsy and learning difficulties. Sheila says she had a 'sneaking suspicion' when he was only weeks old that all was not well. 'He was very floppy, and as he got older he didn't seem to be developing head control. But it was still a terrible shock when we had the diagnosis. I accept he has physical problems – I'd be mad not to – but I believe he's a lot brighter than we've been given to believe. There's a lot going on inside his head.'

Watching the group seated at the plinth, painting with sponges, their mothers beside them, it was obvious that Ben was one of the most handicapped. Sheila had to carry out all the motions for him, holding her hand over his and making sure he was sitting in the right position, keeping his head up and eyes positioned to look ahead.

She found out about the nursery from a physiotherapist who was treating Ben at a local hospital:

> She knew I wanted to do more. An occasional bit of physio can't put everything right. Coming here takes up virtually all my time, but it is much better than being at home doing nothing, or trying to work with Ben on my own. There's companionship here and encouragement. I could send him to school now but I don't want to. I like being involved. I don't want to miss anything that's happening to him.

THE FUTURE

Many schools and therapists are incorporating Conductive Education principles into their work, not as a treatment in itself but as another string to their bow. The Spastics Society is establishing a training centre and teaching service for parents at Rutland House. Children with normal intellectual ability or moderate learning difficulties will be catered for at Ingfield Manor School in Sussex. The Society also plans to open other outreach centres in different parts of the country which will offer 'programmes inspired by Peto'.

GETTING HELP

CONDUCTIVE EDUCATION

Rutland House School,
Elm Bank,
Mapperley Road,
Nottingham NH5 5AJ.
Tel: 0602 621315.

Rapid Action for Conductive Education (RACE) – a parents' pressure group campaigning to bring conductive education to Britain.

Secretary,
155 St. John's Hill,
Battersea,
London SW11 1TQ.

The Foundation for Conductive Education – aims to establish conductive education in the United Kingdom.

University of Birmingham,
P.O. Box 363,
Birmingham B15 2TT.
Tel: 021 414 4947.

The Spastics Society,
Education Division,
840 Brighton Road,
Purley,
Surrey CR2 2BH.
Tel: 081 660 8552.

DOMAN-DELACATO THERAPY

The Kerland Clinic,
Marsh Lane,
Huntworth Gate,
Bridgewater,
Somerset TA6 6LQ.
Tel: 0278 429089.

The British Institute for Brain Injured Children,
Knowle Hall,
Bridgwater,
Somerset TA7 8PJ.
Tel: 0278 684060.

Appendix

GETTING HELP – GENERAL ADDRESSES

ACE – Advisory Centre for Education
18 Victoria Park Square,
London E2 9P3.
Tel: 071 980 4566.

AFASIC – Association of all Speech Impaired Children
347 Central Markets,
London EC1A 9NH.
Tel: 071 236 3632/6487.

Carer's National Association
29 Chilworth Mews,
London W2.
Tel: 071 724 7776.

DIAL – Disabled Information Advice Line
Information on all aspects of handicap and disability. To find local
line contact:

DIAL UK,
Park Lodge,
St. Catherine's Hospital,
Tickhill Road,
Balby,
Doncaster,
S. Yorks DN4 8QN.
Tel: 0302 310123.

Down's Syndrome Association
12–13 Clapham Common Southside,
London SW4 7AA.
Tel: 01 720 0008.

MENCAP – *Royal Society for Mentally Handicapped Children and Adults*
123 Golden Lane,
London EC1Y 0RT.
Tel: 071 454 0454.

National Autistic Society
276 Willesden Lane,
London NW2.
Tel: 071 451 1114.

SENSE – National Deaf Blind and Rubella Association
311 Gray's Inn Road,
London WC1X 8PT.
Tel: 071 278 1005/1000.

Social Security leaflets
Leaflets Unit,
P.O. Box 21,
Stanmore,
Middlesex HA7 1AY.
Tel: Freeline Society Security 0800 666555.

Leaflets available include: Attendance Allowance (N1 205), Help for Handicapped People (HB 1), Invalid Car Allowance (N1 212), Mobility Allowance (N1 211), Payment for Severe Vaccine Damage (HB 3), Severe Disablement Allowance (N1 252), Sick or Disabled? (FB 28).

Scottish Society for Mentally Handicapped Children
13 Elmbank Street,
Glasgow G2 4QA.
Tel: 041 226 4521.

The Spastics Society
12 Park Crescent,
London W1N 4EQ.
Tel: 071 636 5020.

Index

Figures in **bold** refer to case studies

1,000 Mothers Questions Answered

ALL YOU NEED TO KNOW ABOUT CHILDREN FROM CONCEPTION TO SCHOOL

Davina Lloyd & Ann Rushton

From the day you first know that you are pregnant, there is so much to learn, so much to think about. At times you may feel, 'if only there were someone to ask about this . . .' 1,000 MOTHERS QUESTIONS ANSWERED will give you the opportunity to share the questions other mothers have asked, and to learn from the practical and sensitive answers, on subjects such as:

- pregnancy and birth
- weaning and early feeding; faddy eaters
- sibling rivalry, family relationships and friendships
- playgroups, choosing a school, homework
- vaccination, home nursing, accidents and emergencies
- how to get back to work
- . . . and much more!

Designed with the busy mother in mind, the book is organized in an easy-to-use question and answer format, enabling you to turn immediately to the specific area which is concerning you at the time. There is a comprehensive index and many questions are cross-referenced to give you an all-round view of the issue.

Davina Lloyd is the mother of two young children and is Editor of the award-winning magazine Practical Parenting; Ann Rushton is a prolific writer and broadcaster in the field of health and nutrition. Together they offer warm, sympathetic, and above all practical advice on every aspect of motherhood.

The Hyperactive Child

WHAT THE FAMILY CAN DO

Belinda Barnes and Irene Colquhoun

A self-help manual written by parents for parents of hyperactive children, explaining what hyperactivity is, what is causing it and how they can set about dealing with the problems through diet – a varied, wholefood diet entirely free from artificial colourants or additives of any kind.

Based on their own experience the authors suggest ways of handling a hyperactive child and how parents of hyperactive children can get together to help each other. Many hundreds of mothers who have been using these methods have found them successful.

Belinda Barnes runs *Foresight*, the association for the promotion of preconceptual care, and Irene Colquhoun is Chairman of the *Hyperactive Children's Parents Support Group*.

Families and Friends

HOW TO HELP YOUR CHILD ENJOY HAPPY RELATIONSHIPS

Dr John Pearce

A child's early relationships are made within the family, and the love and support of a happy background will make all the difference to your child's ability to make positive, healthy relationships later on – from early school friends to the first teenage crush.

Dr John Pearce shares his vast experience of working with children and families to tell you how to make your family a happy one. Find out:

- why families are so important
- what makes a 'happy family'
- how brothers and sisters can be friends as well as rivals
- what you can do to help the children cope if your marriage fails
- how to deal with your children's friends – sorting the 'good' from the 'bad'
- what to do about 'ganging up' – how to help your child to keep friends without giving in to pressure
- how to cope when boy meets girl

1,000 MOTHERS QUESTIONS ANSWERED	0 7225 2169 3	£6.99 ☐
THE HYPERACTIVE CHILD	0 7225 0883 2	£2.50 ☐
FAMILIES AND FRIENDS	0 7225 1725 4	£2.99 ☐
FOOD: TOO FADDY? TOO FAT?	0 7225 2283 5	£2.99 ☐
FIGHTING, TEASING AND BULLYING	0 7225 1722 X	£2.99 ☐
WORRIES AND FEARS	0 7225 1893 5	£2.50 ☐
BAD BEHAVIOUR	0 7225 1723 8	£2.50 ☐

All these books are available at your local bookseller or can be ordered direct from the publishers.

To order direct just tick the titles you want and fill in the form below:

Name: _____

Address: _____

_____

_____ Postcode: _____

Send to: Thorsons Mail Order, Dept 3E, HarperCollins*Publishers*, Westerhill Road, Bishopbriggs, Glasgow G64 2QT.

Please enclose a cheque or postal order or debit my Visa/Access account –

Credit card no: _____

Expiry date: _____

Signature: _____

– to the value of the cover price plus:

UK & BFPO: Add £1.00 for the first book and 25p for each additional book ordered.

Overseas orders including Eire: Please add £2.95 service charge. Books will be sent by surface mail but quotes for airmail despatches will be given on request.

24 HOUR TELEPHONE ORDERING SERVICE FOR ACCESS/VISA CARDHOLDERS – TEL: **041 772 2281.**